**Practical
School Volunteer
and
Teacher-Aide
Programs**

Practical
School Volunteer
and
Teacher-Aide
Programs

Benjamin DaSilva
and
Richard D. Lucas

Parker Publishing Company, Inc.
West Nyack, New York

©1974 *by*

PARKER PUBLISHING COMPANY, INC.

West Nyack, New York

Library of Congress Cataloging in Publication Data

DaSilva, Benjamin
   Practical school volunteer and teacher-aide
programs.

   Bibliography: p.
   1. Volunteer workers in education. 2. Teachers'
assistants. I. Lucas, Richard D.,   joint
author. II. Title.
LB2844.2.D32   371.1'412   73-16305
ISBN 0-13-693887-6

74-3455

Printed in the United States of America

To the memory of Shirley DaSilva —
a dedicated school volunteer
who will be missed by many.

A Word from the Authors
About the Practical Value of This Book

This book gives administrators and teachers practical guidance in planning and implementing volunteer and teacher-aide programs. It offers specific suggestions and ideas on recruiting, training, and effective use of volunteers and teacher aides.

In every community there are many people who are willing to contribute time and energy to help in the schools. To put such vital resources to work you will need to develop meaningful plans based on your needs and objectives. The major intent of this book is to assist you with these goals in ways that will help you make effective use of teacher aides and school volunteers. Each aspect of the many teacher-aide and school-volunteer programs is discussed and suggested procedures for their successful operation are offered.

The authors stress the importance of choosing a chairman to head your volunteer program. You are given hints on how to contact and recruit volunteers through social functions, letters, news articles, application forms, and other means. Sample letters, press releases, forms, and other materials are included to assist you in your initial efforts.

Activities that volunteers can conduct with students are suggested for various grade levels. The volunteer working with primary-grade children is most helpful to the student as he learns reading, writing, and basic arithmetic skills. Upper-grade children frequently need help in improving study skills and preparing for projects and reports. Even at the high school level volunteers and aides are helpful to both teachers and students. Because the needs and behavior of children at various ages are different, suggestions for classroom aides and volunteers appear in separate chapters for preschool, primary, intermediate, and upper grades.

Using teacher aides and volunteers to relieve the teacher of such duties as the preparation of materials, worksheets, and the duplication of tests and other such items can conserve teacher energy and free them to do other more important work. Volunteers and aides can also be of great help in the library or media center. The maintenance and operation of audio-visual equipment can be handled by them if they are trained for such work. Much of the library routine can be and is successfully being done by many aides throughout the nation.

Trends in curriculum development are leading to a greater emphasis on the individualization of instruction. New learning materials designed to meet the academic and social needs of all students require more one-to-one and small-group emphasis for their successful use. These factors, coupled with the ever-increasing financial demands on the taxpayer, make it more and more difficult for school districts to provide the necessary personnel. It becomes more apparent each day that greater use of paraprofessionals and volunteers is imperative.

Essential to the success of volunteer and aide programs are orientation and training. This book provides you with in-service programs outlining practical ways in which aides and volunteers can help the professional staff in the instructional program, noninstructional tasks, clerical and managerial duties, as well as to provide more enrichment experiences for children.

The teacher is provided with many practical suggestions for the preparation of materials and activities by volunteers or paraprofessionals at all grade levels. They include ideas for working in: math, reading, creative enrichment activities, classroom interest centers, remediation, student research, and many other areas. You will also discover many effective ways in which nonprofessionals can be used to help develop effective cafeteria and playground routines, and assist in supervising other nonclassroom activities. This book also shows how volunteers with special skills in the arts can help students in such pursuits as play production, preparation of art exhibits, and musical productions.

A school volunteer or aide may be helpful in almost any of the various functions that are performed in the school. They are a numerous and largely untapped resource available in any area of the country. How effectively school administrators and teachers recruit and make use of these resources will determine the overall success of your school program and this book will help assure your success in these efforts.

Benjamin DaSilva and Richard D. Lucas

Contents

11

Establishing School Volunteer and Teacher-Aide Programs

/ **1**

The success of volunteer and teacher-aide programs depends greatly upon the effectiveness of a school or school system's recruitment. The purpose of this chapter is to present various ways to identify potential volunteers and establish effective means of communicating to them the interest and need the school has for their services. The process of obtaining teacher aides differs from that of obtaining volunteers. We will discuss the different approaches separately when matters unique to either need to be emphasized.

Sample forms and informational letters are included to help in the recruiting process. Also suggested are some organizational patterns that will expedite the procedures. Such an organizational structure can help one school or an entire community depending upon current needs.

You, the school administrator, are an important factor in helping to establish successful volunteer or teacher-aide programs. The role you assume in the volunteer recruitment process is discussed with special emphasis placed on the need to keep open the lines of communication between the school and volunteers.

ASSESSMENT OF NEEDS

Before embarking on volunteer recruitment, it is important to make an assessment of specific needs and to identify areas where the extra help may be best utilized. This information is essential when seeking volunteers, because it enables the potential helper to know in what capacity he will be working and will guide you in recruiting appropriate candidates.

A typical situation might be one where the class size is such that the teacher needs assistance in providing individual attention for several students. Similar service might be provided with one or more volunteers. Sometimes volunteers or aides are needed to help monitor lunchrooms or playgrounds in order to provide a reasonable, duty-free lunch break or conference time for teachers.

Open learning programs may be dependent, to some extent, upon volunteers to work with various age, interest, or ability groups. In such situations, volunteers might be needed to provide clerical services and help the teachers prepare some of the materials needed for individualized instruction.

PROGRAM CHANGES

As teachers become more proficient in working with youngsters, their planning and procedures become more sophisticated. Attempts are made to tailor the programs to meet the needs of individual students. This requires much extra effort on the part of the teachers as they use a diversity of materials in their programs. A discussion of some of the program changes that could be facilitated by the use of volunteers or aides follows.

One-to-One Instruction

Direct communication between teacher and student has always been considered a desirable condition for learning. In this situation the teacher can elicit a direct response and more easily measure the student's understanding. This condition, however, is very difficult to achieve, especially in a large class. The teacher is responsible for the progress of all the students. In order to provide one-to-one programs, the teacher needs some help in the classroom. Extra hands may be used to assist the students as they attempt to improve their skills.

A reality of the learning process is that youngsters progress at varying rates. It is with this in mind that good teachers attempt to provide for the students as individualized a program as is possible. It is often necessary to utilize the technique of small-group instruction in lieu of a totally individualized approach. This enables the instructor to work with students of similar skills and abilities without having to contend with too wide a range. This instructional technique also necessitates more complex planning, as well as the utilization of a greater variety of materials.

New and More Sophisticated Materials

In recent years educators have been introduced to a much wider selection of programs and materials. These materials have proliferated as the larger corporations have acquired many of the educational publishing concerns. A profusion of new materials and hardware has been made available. The teacher must pick and choose from these offerings very carefully because the quality is not consistently good.

The materials range from the traditional textbook series to such sophisticated devices as self-teaching computers. In between these are programmed texts, filmstrips, film loops, multimedia kits, cassettes, preprinted masters, projectuals, video tapes, workbooks, and paperbacks. To complement this array of software is the vast selection of complicated machinery which the teacher must learn to operate. The materials enable the teachers to have more success in working with their students. The better materials help to make learning more palatable, as well as more meaningful. Frequently, teachers may try several different programs in helping their students achieve success. This requires that they be familiar with many different basal series, as well as the supportive materials that go with them.

A teacher who conscientiously uses these instructional aids finds that he has much follow-up in the form of papers to correct and records to keep. He must also continually peruse and select the material that is to be used in his daily lessons. Volunteers could be most helpful in the capacity of assisting teachers in the correction of papers and recording the results. They may also be given the responsibility for the operation and maintenance of the equipment used in the program.

TEACHER NEED FOR ASSISTANCE

The teacher is required to keep detailed records of student achievement. The abundance of modern learning materials makes an accurate inventory a necessity to insure the smooth flow of these items throughout the building. The preparation of worksheets, transparencies, and other materials are time-consuming tasks that extend the length of the teacher's working day. All of these jobs are basically clerical duties that could be partially assumed by volunteer help.

On a typical day a teacher may be required to assume such roles as a mother, referee, seamstress, counselor, sympathetic listener, judge, policeman, banker, and so on. Many of these duties, although physically and mentally fatiguing, do not require professional training to satisfy the student's needs. Nonprofessionals in the classroom, assisting the teacher, could relieve him of some of the burden.

In addition to the classroom program, a teacher is called upon to supervise children in the lunchroom and on the playground. Within the framework of the legal restrictions, volunteers are capable of providing the teacher with this kind of assistance.

STUDENT NEED FOR ASSISTANCE

The student is confronted with a complexity of tasks that he must successfully accomplish at each level of learn-

Assessment of Needs for Volunteers
(To be completed by the teacher)

Teacher's Name _____

Grade Level _____

Subject Taught _____

Class Size _____

Assistance Required (Please comment)

Tutorial Help _____

_____

Small Group Instruction _____

_____

Materials Preparation _____

_____

Storytelling _____

_____

Clerical Assistance _____

_____

Supervisory Assistance _____

_____

Resource Person _____

   Skill (Please list) _____

   Profession (Please list) _____

Subjects in which volunteer assistance is desired (list below) _____

_____

_____

SAMPLE QUESTIONNAIRE

ing. This challenge to the individual presupposes that he has mastered skills that enable him to achieve his goals. Often a youngster has not mastered these skills and is struggling on the verge of frustration to do just that. He may need just a few minutes of individual help each day in order to experience success. Some days the busy teacher does not reach him and he may flounder helplessly. Extra help in each classroom would diminish the possibility of such an occurrence. Volunteers may work with youngsters in various capacities, several of which are discussed later. The important point made here, however, is that a volunteer helping a student may be the significant factor that determines success or failure in school.

OBTAINING VOLUNTEERS AND AIDES

An important key to successful recruitment of volunteers is to convey the important function they will perform in improving instruction. If specific uses are identified and mentioned in the initial communication, it helps to dispel some of the uncertainties that volunteers may have regarding their possible effectiveness. Many people are reluctant to volunteer because they feel they do not have enough formal training and will not be able to cope with the subject matter taught in today's schools.

An effective means of making potential volunteers aware of the school's interest in their service is through a school newsletter. A simple appeal explaining the program and pointing out the areas of need will usually draw some response from the parent population. A brief explanation of the goals of the volunteer program followed by an appeal for contact by interested parties is a good starting point. This helps the school not only to assess the amount of interest, but to help in planning. If a newsletter is not regularly sent home, a short notice could be substituted to accomplish the same purpose. A tear-off sheet at the end of the notice is useful in gathering information from the parents.

Dear Parents:

We are in need of interested people to work in the school as volunteers. As a school volunteer you will help children and their teachers in many important ways.

Volunteers serve as another pair of hands in the library, as listeners to beginning readers, as storytellers, as one-to-one tutors, and in many other ways.

To be a volunteer you need no special skills or experience. All you need is a desire to work with children and a willingness to give a precious gift of time each week — even an hour or two. Please come and be a part of the educational process.

If you are interested in learning more about becoming a school volunteer, please complete the attached form and return it to the school.

Thank you,

_____

Chairman, School Volunteers

BD:hp
Enc.

_ _

FIFTH AVENUE SCHOOL VOLUNTEER PROGRAM

Name: _____

Address: _____

Phone: _____

Days and time available:

	Mon.	Tues.	Wed.	Thurs.	Fri.
a.m.	____	____	____	_____	___
p.m.	____	____	____	_____	___

SAMPLE RECRUITING LETTER FROM THE
SCHOOL BUILDING CHAIRMAN TO PARENTS

Meetings with parent groups may be useful in making initial contact. Groups might be invited into the school in the evening or during the day for coffee and an opportunity to discuss volunteer procedures and to have any questions answered. Demonstration lessons conducted by staff members at these sessions help to give parents a clearer indication of the function of a school volunteer. An opportunity for questions and responses should also be provided at the conclusion of such sessions.

Teachers, in the course of their daily relationships with parents, may be helpful in identifying potential volunteers. They are in excellent position to know those people who may be readily recruited to work with children. The principal also has much contact with the parent group and should be alert to possible candidates.

Good volunteers are often parents who have shown much interest in the school and have supported activities in the past. Your making personal contacts with these people and inviting them to participate in the volunteer program is a good way to get the recruiting off to a successful beginning.

PARENT-TEACHER GROUPS

Most schools have parent-teacher organizations which have all the prerequisites necessary for assisting in the process of obtaining volunteers. P.T.A. meetings could be devoted to discussion of volunteer programs and to inform the parent body of the specific needs of the school.

P.T.A. officers are usually willing to help in recruiting. A chairman of volunteers chosen from this group could assume the responsibility of coordinating the activities of the parent workers. Close liaison between school personnel and the volunteer chairman is necessary to keep open the lines of communication.

Preparing a brochure that explains the role of the volunteer may help to stimulate interest. Such a brochure should describe: what a volunteer does in the classroom; how they can be helpful in supervisory situations; what the needs of the school are for volunteer help; how the children will be benefited; help to allay fears regarding the amount of training necessary for this type of work; explain that the school is flexible and will help parents fit the program into their schedule; offer a choice of areas in which they may work; and explain any other aspects of the program which may be unique to a particular school. An application form should accompany the brochure.

ORGANIZATIONAL PATTERNS
FOR VOLUNTEER PROGRAMS

The structure of organization varies with the needs of the school or the community. It is also dependent upon the type of program to be instituted. A program involving the use of volunteers to assist in classroom instruction in a given school usually is headed by one volunteer leader who helps in the recruiting of parent workers. This person meets with the principal and teachers and follows up on their request for assistance. The chairman keeps a list of active volunteers and helps to place them in classrooms. She may also take the responsibility for finding substitutes if needed.

SAMPLE RECRUITING BROCHURE

TO: All Interested Members of the Community

FROM: Chairman of School Volunteers

There is a great opportunity for interested adults to serve the schools as volunteers. A school volunteer may be of assistance in a variety of ways. If you have the time to lend a helping hand in the schools and are interested in working with children, your services are very much needed. No special skills are required to enroll as a volunteer. You will receive some preservice training prior to your placement in a school. The personal rewards are countless!

School volunteers are needed to work in the following areas:

LIBRARY/MEDIA
CENTERS:
Volunteers provide valuable assistance in student research projects, study skills, and efficient use of library resources on the elementary, junior and senior high school levels.

STORYTELLING:
Volunteers tell and read stories to individual children or small groups selected by the classroom teacher, for enrichment, recreation, and language arts development.

ENGLISH AS A
A SECOND
LANGUAGE:
Volunteers, working with two or three children at a time, help foreign-speaking children feel at home and acquire some of the language skills so vital to their progress in learning.

PERFORMING
ARTS:
Volunteers bring professional performances in theater, music, and dance to all children without charge.

ONE-TO-ONE:
Volunteers provide a variety of individual attention for children with special needs through tutoring and friendship.

ART AND MUSIC
EXPERIENCES:
Volunteers provide appropriate slide lectures (with student participation) in Early American, Renaissance, Impressionists to Contemporary, and present day American art. Talks on the various music forms are given accompanied by recorded music.

HEAD START
AND SPECIAL
EDUCATION:
Volunteers assist in Head Start and special education classes in various ways.

STUDENT-TO-
STUDENT:
College and high school students work with elementary school children on an individual basis as tutors as well as "big brothers" and "big sisters."

CLERICAL
ASSISTANCE:
To give teachers added time with students by providing nonteaching, clerical assistance.

If you are interested in serving as a volunteer in any of these areas, please notify your building representative, or you can call the school office. The chairman for your school is: (list schools and chairman)

_____

SAMPLE VOLUNTEER APPLICATION FORM
Name of School District

School Volunteer Application

Date:_____Source of Referral_____

Name: _____Spouse's name _____
      last   first

Address: _____Telephone_____

Age: Under 20_____21-40_____ 41-60_____Over 60__

Education: High School_____ College_____ Other_____

Work Experience:

Specific Job	How Long Employed
_____	_____
_____	_____
_____	_____

Volunteer Experience:

Organization	Job	Length of Service
_____	_____	_____
_____	_____	_____

Children: Number:_____ Ages:_____

Schools Attending:_____

Special skills such as: Art, dramatics, handicrafts, writing, musical instruments, publicity, singing, stenography, typing, languages.

Specify skill (s): _____ Others _____

Days and times available:

	Mon.	Tues.	Wed.	Thurs.	Fri.
a.m.	____	____	____	____	____
p.m.	____	____	____	____	____

Person to be notified in emergency _____

Telephone_____

References: Two persons unrelated to you who have known you for at least two years.

NAME: _____ ADDRESS: _____

NAME: _____ ADDRESS: _____

Assignment preferred:

_____

The chairman helps to coordinate volunteers working in different areas, e.g., library volunteers, classroom assistants, clerical helpers, supervisory aides. This person also assists the school administration in any communication necessary with the volunteers and may help in the planning of preservice or in-service workshops.

The principal, as the overseer of the volunteer force in his school, should hold periodic meetings with volunteers and teachers. A major responsibility is to see that the volunteers have adequate space in which to work with children and are scheduled to fit smoothly into the school environment.

The teacher is a most important element in the organizational pattern because it is his responsibility to see that the volunteer is used effectively and to the benefit of the students. He must prepare work assignments and select students to meet with the volunteer. The teacher must be cognizant of the fact that the volunteer is not a professional and is dependent upon professional guidance to provide optimum service to the students.

This school-level organization consisting of principal, teacher, chairman of volunteers, and individual workers should be looked upon as a team effort whose primary goal is to improve the learning atmosphere. Each member must be aware of his role and his responsibility. The encouragement of intragroup communication on a continual basis helps to improve the effectiveness of the volunteer effort.

COMMUNITY-WIDE
VOLUNTEER ORGANIZATIONAL PATTERNS

Many school systems find much value in establishing a community-wide volunteer program. One person assumes the role of chairman of volunteers and coordinates the activities of the various school volunteer chairmen. In some instances this may be a paid position, but is most often a volunteer assignment. The chairman has as his or her duties:

1. Selection of individual school chairmen
2. Organization of training workshops
3. Publicizing of volunteer programs
4. Recruitment of new volunteers
5. Liaison with central office personnel
6. Liaison with other community volunteer agencies
7. Locating groups that provide enrichment programs for schools
8. Any other task having town-wide implications

There is a built-in efficiency to a community organization in that it eliminates the need for duplication of efforts in the individual schools. Recruitment, publicity, and training may be done more effectively if they are the responsibility of one segment of the volunteer effort. Workshops can be run in a centralized area and may be designed to accommodate larger numbers.

In a community-wide structure the school organizational pattern remains essentially the same. The building workers, freed from some of their nonteaching tasks, can concentrate on improving the instructional process.

SYSTEM-WIDE SCHOOL VOLUNTEER PROGRAMS

Some programs are more suitable to system-wide organization. Most of these are discussed in greater detail in later chapters, but are mentioned here as part of the organizational scheme. Any activity that involves interschool or community groups is best coordinated by a system-wide agency. A program such as student-to-student tutors involving junior or senior high school students working with elementary school pupils is one example. Others are art appreciation groups, dramatic groups, tutoring programs, English as a second language volunteers, and story hour groups.

A community resource file may also be developed for use in all the schools. Such a file would list volunteer citizens who have special skills, knowledge, and experiences, which cover many kinds of careers and avocations, that they would like to share with children and that the school feels will be helpful in its efforts. The compiling of this list is an arduous task. Undertaken by one agency it can then be duplicated and shared by each of the schools.

In short, wherever it is feasible to do so, it would be more desirable for you to organize along community lines and thus eliminate the need for repetition of efforts in each school.

SCHOOL VOLUNTEER PROGRAM

If you can spare one, two, or more hours each week to help children, your services as a school volunteer are being sought by the School Volunteer Program.

Volunteers perform a variety of activities such as: reading to children, listening to them read, one-to-one tutoring, assisting in the library, and in many other ways. Skill is not required. All that is asked is a willingness to work with children. "Often, that little extra time and attention a volunteer can provide may be just enough to help a child get the most out of school," the volunteer leaders report.

Those interested are asked to contact the school office in their district. The Volunteer Program is interested in new volunteers from all walks of life and age groups.

SAMPLE NEWS RELEASE

TEACHER-AIDE PROGRAMS
What Is a Teacher Aide?

A teacher aide is a paraprofessional person employed to assist in the educational efforts of a school. They are paraprofessional in the sense that it is not their primary responsibility to innovate or initiate instruction. They are assistants who take direction from you, the teacher, principal, or supervisor, in an effort to extend the effectiveness of the learning process. They are not substitute teachers and should not, as a rule, be expected to take over major responsibilities of a classroom teacher. An aide is a very important resource who, when effectively utilized, can help you do a more thorough job of educating students.

Obtaining Teacher Aides

Teacher aides may be found in a manner similar to that of locating volunteers. A good source of aides is from among the parent group of a school. The advantage of seeking aides from within the school family is that the administration has some insight into the capabilities of the candidate. It is also helpful to the potential aide to have prior knowledge of the school program and its philosophy.

Parent organizations again may be useful in helping to obtain teacher-aide candidates. Members of the group may be approached through personal contact, written communication, or at regular meetings. The school administration may wish to communicate the need for aide candidates by sending notices to homes. If this is done, the communication should contain a brief explanation of the job plus a list of the criteria by which selection will be made. Information regarding method of application should also be included.

When aides are hired on a community-wide basis, advertisements may be placed in a local newspaper. This is not feasible for a single school unless there are not enough good candidates available from among the parent group.

Organizational Patterns for Teacher-Aide Programs

Teacher-aide programs may be organized in a manner similar to that of a volunteer program. In a single school the principal assumes the major responsibilities for hiring and placing the aides. Teachers who will be assigned aides, however, should take part in the hiring process. Evaluation of aides should be a co-responsibility of the principal and the participating teacher. Since aides are paid employees, there should be a job description for their assignment. They also must be held accountable for the satisfactory dispatch of their obligations, as are other members of the educational process.

When aide programs are organized on a community-wide basis, a coordinator is usually employed. This person has the responsibility of recruiting and hiring candidates, establishing training programs, placing aides, and supervising their activities. The principals and teachers should also share these responsibilities much as they do when only a single school is involved. Having a coordinator to help in the recruiting and hiring of aides helps to expedite the process. Public relations concerning the teacher-aide program is a co-responsibility of the individual schools and the office of the coordinator.

CRITERIA FOR HIRING PARAPROFESSIONALS

Teacher aides, being paid employees, and often serving in a full-time capacity, should be selected with the same careful consideration you give to hiring professional staff members. Aides usually work very closely with students, hence they must possess the qualities necessary to assure a positive and meaningful educational relationship. When hiring paraprofessionals, it is necessary to establish criteria which help to guide you in making your selection. Some of the desirable qualities are as follows:

1. *An interest in working with children.* The aide must be motivated by more than just a desire for gainful employment. She must be interested in children and have a sincere desire to work with them in the learning process. She should be responsive to the needs of school-age children and work to establish rapport with her students.

2. *Possess good communication skills.* The paraprofessional needs to be able to communicate effectively with both the students and the classroom teacher. Communication implies listening as well

as speaking. An aide who is a good listener will gain the confidence of the teacher as well as the cooperation of her students. The aide must be able to speak clearly and at a level of understanding of the students.

3. *Be dependable in her job function.* A good aide must follow through on instructions from the teacher or supervisor, be on time, and avoid unnecessary absenteeism. A dependable aide also shows concern for the welfare of her students by being consistent in the quality of her relationship with them.

4. *Display stability in the classroom.* Stability of temperament is important in gaining the confidence and respect of the students. An aide with erratic behavior patterns and frequent emotional highs and lows can be very unsettling to the learning atmosphere.

5. *Loyalty to the school.* An aide who is disenchanted with the school program can have a negative effect in both the classroom and in the community. It is important to seek people who are familiar with and supportive of the school's philosophy. Since the teacher aides do not have the same degree of autonomy in a classroom as the teacher, they could be frustrated if they do not believe in the methods being employed.

6. *Show discretion in communicating with parents.* An aide has the same responsibility as a teacher for discreet behavior in regard to discussing her students. A youngster's progress or lack of it must not be a topic of conversation for neighborhood gatherings. When an aide discusses a child's progress with his parents, she must not go beyond the bounds of her own expertise.

7. *Willingness to take direction.* The nature of the position of teacher aide requires that the person be directable. An aide is dependent upon the teach-

er to establish the educational techniques that are to be used. If the personality is such that the aide finds it difficult to take direction from another person, then conflict is likely to result. There will be many opportunities for the aide to employ her own creativity within the structure devised by the professional staff members.

8. *Be of sound health.* An aide should be sufficiently healthy to permit her to meet her obligations. Health examinations before and throughout service should be required.

9. *Be willing to attend a training program.* Some formal training in the nature of a workshop or short course of study is a necessary prerequisite to prepare the paraprofessional for her position. The good aide knows that training is an ongoing, never-ending part of education.

10. *Be reasonably free from excessively time-consuming home responsibilities.* An aide who has small children or infirm relatives at home must make adequate plans for their welfare so that her home responsibilities will not seriously interfere with her regular performance.

SCREENING CANDIDATES AND THE INTERVIEW

An application that requires sufficient information about the candidate is useful for the screening process. Such an application would resemble that used for volunteers as shown earlier in this chapter. The early screening procedure will help you to determine those candidates you wish to interview.

At least one interview with a teacher-aide candidate should be conducted at the school. Teachers who will be working with the paraprofessional should participate in the interview. Even when aides are hired through a coordinator, the people with building-level responsibility should be involved in the selections.

Once you have organized an effective and ongoing recruiting program, you must be alert to the need for modification and improvement based on needs. The communication that takes place between school and the community is the key to the successful initiation of a volunteer or teacher-aide program.

Remember that a well-organized program includes professional as well as volunteer leaders who assume responsibility for its operation. Beyond the school level a program organized on a community-wide basis helps to extend the effectiveness of such an operation and to make it more efficient by eliminating the need to duplicate tasks at the building level.

Training Volunteers and Teacher Aides / 2

If programs that employ the services of volunteers or teacher aides are to succeed in the school, it is important that proper training and orientation of the participants take place. Teachers who have not worked with volunteers or aides are frequently hesitant to begin doing so. Until the staff in a school becomes comfortable with the working procedures, there may be instances of misunderstanding, confusion, and hurt feelings. Proper groundwork will prevent this and help you to set the stage for a productive relationship in which the children are the benefactors.

ORIENTING TEACHERS TO THE VOLUNTEER AND TEACHER-AIDE PROGRAMS

When either a teacher-aide or volunteer program is instituted, you must be sure the goals and objectives of the programs in your school are clearly understood. The initial introduction can take place at a regular staff meeting. At this meeting it is important that a clear overall picture is presented, and that there is an opportunity for staff questions and discussion. If the staff is involved throughout the planning stages, this will not be a major task. If there was little input by the staff throughout the development, it may be necessary to hold a series of informative meetings.

Once the staff has been introduced to the concept of a teacher-aide or volunteer program and knows the goals, one or more workshops should be planned. At these workshops teachers will learn of the many ways in which paraprofessionals can be an asset to them. Many of their fears will be allayed when they come to realize that the paraprofessionals with whom they come in contact will have been trained in ways to provide teachers with valuable assistance. At these workshops specific activities that can be conducted by the paraprofessional should be demonstrated and discussed.

Teachers may be encouraged to visit classes in other communities or districts that employ teacher aides or have an extensive volunteer program. Some of the ideas they gain may benefit your program for they may observe activities and techniques that you have not yet considered. It may be stated here that a good orientation program for teachers about to participate in a teacher-aide or volunteer program can produce many side benefits. In the process of learning how aides and volunteers benefit the classroom, many teachers will gain practical ideas and valuable insights into modern approaches toward the individualization of instruction.

In-Service Training of Volunteers

When considering the training of volunteers, one must think of them in slightly different terms than teacher aides. Volunteers are usually, but not always, parents who are eager and willing to perform a public service without remuneration. Some will be eager to spend a great deal of time in the school each week; others may be able to devote only one or two hours in a single day each week. The school should be prepared to accommodate such a flexible schedule. The staff must also recognize that some volunteers may be absent more often than someone who is part of the paid staff. To prevent this, care must be taken in the volunteer training program to stress the importance of punctuality and regularity of attendance. Volunteers should know that excessive absenteeism is harmful to steady progress of children and weakens their relationship with them.

There are many methods and procedures that volunteers will need to follow in the various activities in which they engage. There are, however, some general principles that should be observed for all activities. For example: (1) Care must be taken to insure that the adult communicates on the vocabulary and comprehension level of the children with whom he or she works. (2) The adult volunteer should avoid correcting serious infractions of discipline. She must consult the professional. (3) The volunteer must not embark on new areas, subjects, or methods without the full knowledge and consent of the professional staff involved.

When training volunteers the professional staff must make a careful effort to explain the needs of the children with whom the volunteer will work. If the child or children assigned to a volunteer give evidence of a need for affection and emotional reinforcement, you must make the volunteer aware of this. Building trust can be more significant than academic gains at certain times in a child's development. You will need to provide volunteers with a general description of the emotional makeup of the children with whom they will work, as well as an explanation of their school needs.

Volunteers should know the objectives of the school as well as those of the teachers. If they have a general knowledge of the direction in which the school and individual classrooms are moving, it will be easier for them to understand their place in the total program. This effort must be renewed as new volunteers are added to the program.

We often think parents are up-to-date on school matters because their children attend our schools. Unfortunately, this is not always the case. When considering the school, adults often think in terms of their own childhood experiences.

As a part of their training volunteers should be encouraged to observe teachers working with children. This must be planned so that the volunteers will benefit from their visit. You will want to be sure that the volunteer observes teachers when they are actively engaged in meaningful work. After the parent has observed different teachers in varying activities, an opportunity should be provided for them to discuss what they saw, ask questions, and be guided in understanding the role of the teacher.

All schools have general rules that apply to students as well as to professional staff. They may be quite specific in some instances, and very general in others. It is important that volunteers know these rules, which may pertain to such matters as arrival and dismissal times, areas for smoking, use of toilet facilities, and lounge and lunchroom accommodations. An understanding of these rules can prevent much confusion and misunderstanding as volunteers work in the schools.

While it may be necessary for the principal or teacher to be tactful when discussing the need for volunteers to be punctual and dependable, it is important that this subject be covered. The volunteer must be made to realize that the relationship he builds with children is of great significance. The child must not be made to feel that he is less important than hairdressing appointments and Christmas shopping. If you know that participation on the part of some volunteers will be occasional and sporadic, it might be wiser to discourage this person from participation, or to engage him in volunteer activities that do not require continuity or regularity.

While the above suggestions can provide some basic guidelines for volunteers, they have been somewhat general. When a parent has decided upon the specific activity he wishes to engage in, you must make an effort to adapt these guidelines to this activity and identify in detail the skills and methodology employed. As an example, if the volunteer is interested in a reading-tutoring activity, it is incumbent on you to provide good opportunities for observation. discussion with reading or regular classroom teachers, a careful explanation of the individual needs of the children who will be involved, as well as practical demonstrations of the desired methodology.

PRESERVICE AND IN-SERVICE TRAINING
OF TEACHER AIDES

After the school has determined its needs for teacher-aide programs and has selected people who will participate, it faces the important task of providing meaningful training.

While many of the elements of a good training program for aides resemble those of a volunteer program, there are distinct differences. A teacher aide, like a volunteer, may be employed to do a specific job, but the aide will, in most cases, be involved in work with children for more hours each day and each week. They will be subjected to many facets of child behavior and be a part of the learning process for a more sustained period. It must be remembered that once a person becomes a paid member of the staff, his position is of a more permanent nature than that of a volunteer. You will want to be sure that the aide has the help necessary to insure a good beginning.

As was true with the volunteer training, aides should receive a thorough review of the major programs that exist in the school. They should also learn of the goals and objectives of the school and its teachers. Even the most conscientious aides can begin to look upon their function as more vital than the rest of the school's operation if they do not see their role in its proper perspective.

Some effective teacher-aide programs owe much of their success to a formalized prescribed training course for teacher-aide applicants before and during their service. A course of this nature might culminate in the granting of a certificate or diploma and result in an increase in pay or elevation to the regular salary scale established for teacher aides.

This course should involve, as instructors, highly skilled members of your staff. Lessons and activities must be carefully planned, because what is demonstrated and taught sets the stage for future success. In some communities the task of aide training is part of the community adult education program. Listed here are some suggested topics for such a course or training program.

Feelings Come First

A session or sessions should be devoted to building in aides an understanding of their feelings regarding themselves, other adults and children. Many of the current "sensitivity" or encounter techniques may be employed. Many aides who have been through a program like this have indicated that they were able to look upon their own children and family situations in a new light. Sessions like these coming at the beginning of a program do much to insure an atmosphere in which there is involvement throughout the course.

Role of the Teacher

During the sessions in which the teacher's role is covered, it must be stressed that in most instances the teacher serves the role of the "senior partner" while maintaining the spirit of a team effort. In this capacity, the teacher delegates responsibility without abdicating responsibility. It is important that aides realize that the ultimate or final decisions must and should be made by the professional staff.

Role of the Principal or Supervisor

The new aides must understand that those with supervisory responsibility must observe and criticize those activities that take place under their jurisdiction. A principal wants his school to run efficiently. He, more than anyone, is able to see the overall operation of the school and make judgments regarding how individuals contribute to the professional life of the school. While the principal or supervisor serves in the capacity of a "boss," aides should be encouraged to freely discuss their problems and observations of children with him. Often an aide's one-to-one proximity to a child can provide valuable assistance to even the best and most perceptive professional staff members who are engaged in many activities and work with larger numbers of children.

Child Development

Several sessions should be devoted to this vital area. Efforts must be made to explain such concepts as I.Q., maturity levels, interest spans, and so on. A discussion of the various levels of muscle development and coordination is also needed. Careful analysis of what motivates children at different stages of development is important. Aides who have not lived in deprived neighborhoods or similar situations should learn of the many social forces at work that determine behavior patterns at school. The importance of a child's environment in determining success at school should be aired thoroughly.

Special Programs

At least one session should be held on each special program such as art, music, physical education, and preschool Head Start. A very helpful approach can be to utilize specialists in these areas in actual lessons comparable to those taught to the children. The music teacher might teach a new song or two; the art teacher might conduct an art project that would call upon the participants' creative abilities. After such sessions are held, it is helpful to repeat the lesson with an actual group of children having the trainees study the behavior and skills of the children as compared to those of the adults. If those being trained will be used more extensively in programs such as Head Start or preschool, you will, of course, need to concentrate more intensively on activities emphasized in these programs.

The Library/Media Center

Each year the media center becomes more and more identified as the heart of a school operation. As more space for this facility is provided and more varied materials added, it becomes a highly sophisticated operation. Sessions should be held to explain the procedures in modern library/media centers as well as to study the many and varied materials. These sessions would more profitably be held in the actual facility.

Media Materials

Class sessions should be conducted on the operation of media equipment. It is important that aides not only see demonstrated such devices as the overhead projector, 16 mm movie projector, and the many new audio-visual devices, but they must also actively participate in the operation of these machines. A helpful way to provide the actual experience would be to set up a room in which stations are established. Each station would feature the operation of a machine or device. As each participant becomes familiar with its operation, he would move to the next station and then the next. The stations could be conducted by volunteers, teachers, or experienced students. It is an excellent activity for children who assist in their schools' audio-visual program.

Storytelling and the Language Arts Program

We will discuss the many ways in which aides can assist the language arts and reading program in future chapters. During the training program it is important, especially for those who will participate in any phase of language arts, that the participants study the programs and techniques used by the schools. Telling and reading stories to the group can provide excellent practice. In developing skills in these activities it is often advisable to engage those members of the class who are more extroverted.

Testing and Keeping Records

This session should include an explanation of why the various standardized and individual tests are administered to children and what they tell the school. If aides are to participate in the administration of tests, they must learn the basic guidelines for testing. The guidance counselor can be helpful in this discussion. Like the parents of students, aides may have many misconceptions about the various I.Q. and aptitude tests administered and what the scores mean. This session should correct these misunderstandings. The discussion must also center around the need for discretion when observing and recording scores.

First Aid

In some communities aides are given a minicourse on first aid as part of their total training. This is highly desirable for aides on any level. Numerous times they have provided an excellent service when a school nurse was not available. Often they will know more about what to do in cases of emergency than teachers who have had no training and little experience in such matters.

Paraprofessional Ethics

Time must be spent on the important subject of ethics. The aide must know that information gained on children, as well as staff members, should not be conveyed to those who do not function in the school setting. Idle gossip outside of the school, as well as within the school, can often create an atmosphere that is not conducive to a good educational setting. As those in the medical and legal professions are trained to observe a code of ethics regarding privileged information, so must the educational paraprofessional recognize this need.

SUPERVISION OF TEACHER AIDES AND VOLUNTEERS

As teacher aides begin to apply in the classroom what they have learned from their training, supervision is an important next step. If it is possible for a school system to employ a full-time professional to assume this role, so much the better. In many instances this responsibility will be primarily that of the principal and the teacher involved. Like teachers, aides profit most from professional assistance and supervision in the early formative years of their work.

Throughout the training of teacher aides and volunteers and their subsequent ongoing supervision, it is most essential that positive attitudes are developed. The paraprofessional should feel that working with children is a noble endeavor and an opportunity to develop one's creative abilities. He should feel that training never ends and that self-improvement in our efforts on behalf of educating children is a constant goal that can provide rich personal reward.

The professional staff can do much to foster an atmosphere in which a positive attitude prevails. In schools where the teachers and administrators exhibit an abundance of energy, friendliness, and a sincere interest in the development of children, the aides will undoubtedly reflect this spirit.

We have suggested some measures to enable you to develop the necessary training programs that will help to insure a successful volunteer or teacher-aide program. You will need to adapt some of the ideas to fit the needs of your school and the talents of the people who come to help. It must be remembered that the paraprofessional who is best prepared will be most effective. This preparation must provide an understanding of the school needs, a knowledge of children and how they learn, and a reasonable degree of competence in the methods required by the activities. While much assistance is provided to you, the educators, in the execution of their work, added responsibility must also be yours to insure an atmosphere in which creative and cooperative efforts are continually made on behalf of children.

TRAINING WORKSHOPS IN CONTENT AREAS

Demonstration workshops as a part of the training program could prove very effective in providing volunteers and aides with skills and techniques for working with students. The format of a workshop is such that you can provide instruction in a content area and demonstrate good teaching techniques at the same time.

Most nonprofessional school volunteers are frightened by the prospect of helping youngsters in modern math. They feel it is so totally different from the traditional arithmetic they are familiar with that it would be difficult for them to assist the students. There are other areas of volunteer concern that could be used as a basis for a workshop during the training program. The selection of such topics is dependent upon your needs and how you plan to use volunteers in your school.

A workshop designed to improve the volunteer's or aide's skills in a specific area should be of fairly short duration. Most volunteers do not have an abundance of time to devote to this sort of activity. A program scheduled for one-half hour sessions for four days or for a four-hour session in one day should be sufficient to provide the volunteers or aides with enough confidence to work with students. A typical four-day workshop could consist of the following:

First Day — Introduction to Modern Math

It would be well, by way of introduction, to explain the concept of modern math to the volunteer-aides. This program is unfamiliar to most adults and frequently they are not familiar with the rationale for converting to the new math as opposed to the more traditional programs. It is not necessary to prepare a dissertation on the relative merits of the newer innovations in math. A brief survey of the new terminology and the major concepts would be useful in orienting the volunteer-aides to the math program.

Materials.   Modern math uses many materials such as: texts, workbooks, math games, worksheets, flashcards, filmstrips, tapes, and projectuals. These are the basic tools with which the volunteers and aides will assist the students in the learning process. They should be familiar with these materials and be aware of the function of each in the acquisition of math skills.

Review of Basic Skills.   A review of the basic math skills — addition, subtraction, multiplication, and division — would be helpful in refreshing the volunteer. It is, of course, not necessary to reteach these skills, but rather, merely to summarize the rules and processes involved. If the assistants are to work with older students, it is necessary to review such areas as fractions and decimals.

Second Day — Practice in Modern Math

Use of Manipulative Materials.   Some of the basic number functions in modern math are best demonstrated through the use of manipulative materials. These materials, which come in various forms, are described in more detail in other chapters. The volunteers and aides would benefit from the opportunity of practicing techniques for using these materials.

It should be pointed out to the trainees that they can be most helpful in the process of collecting items to be used in the instruction of math.

Practice in Sets and Bases. A few exercises designed to familiarize the volunteers and aides with the concepts of sets and bases would be a useful technique. These should be simple introductory lessons that can help to give confidence to the volunteer. An important fact to remember is that nonprofessionals usually are not called upon to teach these skills. Their function will be mainly that of assistance to the student.

Practice Basic Number Functions. By way of refreshing the volunteers, it would be helpful to prepare a few worksheets on the basic number functions. These sheets should contain a brief review of the procedures used in addition, subtraction, division, and multiplication. This could be followed by some worksheets featuring a series of review exercises.

Third Day — Material Preparation

A service frequently performed by an aide or a volunteer is to assist the teacher in the preparation of materials. This assistance may come in the form of worksheet transparency or mimeo stencil preparation, as well as in the actual machine operation for reproduction.

Part of the time should be devoted to a demonstration of the proper procedures for preparing: (1) a spirit master, (2) a mimeo stencil, and (3) an overhead transparency. The different application for each student should be explained. Sample copies of each type of worksheet would be helpful in the discussion.

Demonstration of Equipment. Volunteers or aides frequently perform the service of running off copies of duplicated materials. They must be familiar with the operation of such pieces of equipment as a photocopier, spirit duplicator, mimeograph machine, or master maker. After demonstrating the proper method of operation for each piece of equipment, it would be helpful to allow each trainee to practice with the machines.

Fourth Day — Practice Tutoring

On the final day of the workshop you may wish to have the group pair off and practice tutoring one another. You can prepare worksheets for this purpose. This exercise will help to sharpen skills as well as to inspire confidence in the volunteer or aide.

It would be helpful to culminate the workshop by summarizing the activities. A question-answer session would give the volunteers and aides the opportunity to clear up any points of uncertainty. Your final words of encouragement should prepare the volunteers or aides for their new role as a part of the educational process.

SAMPLE WORKSHOP ON AUDIO-VISUAL EQUIPMENT

A workshop on the operation of audio-visual equipment would be useful to new volunteers or aides. They are often called upon to operate the various machines and they should be familiar with the correct procedures. A three-day workshop consisting of three one-hour sessions would consist of the following activities.

First Day — Demonstration of Equipment

The audio-visual equipment most likely to be used by a volunteer or aide includes a movie projector, filmstrip projector, tape recorder, phonograph, and an overhead projector. You should have this equipment available as you describe the function of each. A brief description of the apparatus would include some discussion of its use in a classroom. There are films available to help in this presentation.

As a part of the demonstration you should use each piece of equipment as it would be used in an actual lesson. For example, you could prepare an overhead projection transparency to show the many uses of that instrument.

Observation of Equipment. The volunteers and aides should be given the opportunity to handle the equipment. At this time they may have some questions about the function of the various pieces of apparatus. This part of the day's session need only be approximately ten minutes in length. The second day of the workshop will give the trainees a much closer look at the equipment.

Second and Third Days — Operating Instructions

The best procedures for training the volunteers and aides in the operation of the audio-visual equipment is the use of small groups. Divide the class into five groups. Each of these groups will be taught the proper method of operation for the machines. This instruction should include verbal information as well as an actual demonstration. The groups move from one place to another until they have received instructions on each piece of equipment.

"Hands On" Training. The trainees must be given the opportunity to practice with the audio-visual equipment. It is the actual operation of these machines that will give the volunteers and aides the confidence they need to be helpful in the classroom.

It is doubtful that this training can be completed in one day. You will probably need two full sessions to give each volunteer the opportunity to work with each piece of equipment. It would be wise to assess the needs of each trainee and provide extra help to those individuals in need of it.

Fourth Day — Simple Maintenance Procedures

There are many maintenance tasks that can be performed by volunteers or aides. These include such things as bulb replacement, lens cleaning, light oiling, fuse replacement, belt and pulley tightening, and repairing cords. If the trainees are encouraged to practice good preventive maintenance, the operating life of the equipment will be prolonged.

It is always useful to conclude a workshop with a review of the highlights of the week's activities. A short quiz, either oral or written, would help to pull things together and serve as a culmination of the fourth session.

Using Volunteers and Aides in Libraries or Media Centers

School libraries have long been in the forefront of the school volunteer programs. In many communities it has been necessary to use volunteers in order to operate school libraries. Before the library became established as an essential part of the elementary school, mobile libraries organized by volunteer help were commonly used.

Now that many elementary schools have a regular library, volunteers can still be called upon to provide many useful functions. In this chapter we suggest many ways that volunteers and teacher aides can be helpful in the library. These include such far-ranging tasks as shelf arrangement and book repair to actual operation of a library where a professional librarian is not available.

Volunteers provide the librarian with the extra help necessary to keep a smooth-running facility that provides maximum support to the school program. They might be used strictly as assistants who sign out and replace books on the shelves or they might work with the students in a more direct way.

Storytelling and discussion groups are activities that can be successfully carried on by volunteers. Whether volunteers and aides are needed in a primary or secondary role, there are many ways in which they can be useful in the operation of a school library.

Part of this chapter is devoted to suggestions for using volunteers and aides in school media centers. In recent years as media technology has developed and been incorporated into the library, the school resource center has become increasingly important. Opportunities for providing expanded services through the use of volunteers and aides are many and varied.

Volunteers and aides may monitor student use of equipment and assist them in its use. They may be responsible for the flow of hardware and software that is borrowed for use outside of the media center. Filing and record keeping are tasks easily assumed by volunteers and aides. Trained assistants may be able to perform routine maintenance on the equipment, which could save expensive repair costs.

As the school library and media center become more sophisticated and complex, there is a burgeoning need for greater help in the successful operation of these facilities.

SCHOOL VOLUNTEERS ASSISTING IN
LIBRARY ROUTINES

Volunteers, with very little training, may be used to assume some of the routine, but time-consuming, tasks of library operation. The process of signing out books is a good example of this. A volunteer used for this purpose frees the trained librarian to work more directly with the students in the teaching of library skills.

Volunteers can check books in and out and keep abreast of the overdue books. They may be responsible for replacing returned books on the shelves. Library shelves need constant attention to keep them properly arranged. Card files need maintenance and updating. Volunteers can assist the librarian in cataloguing new acquisitions to the collection. This is a job that requires great expenditures of time in typing and filing. If volunteers are trained to assume some of these responsibilities, the librarian can be free to perform instructional functions. Often teachers request that a reserve shelf on a specific subject be set aside for their use. The library teacher may make the selections and then rely on a volunteer or aide to actually collect the books and set up the shelf.

Book repair is another useful operation that may be handled by volunteers. A brief training period and provision of appropriate materials is all that is needed to carry on this activity. A book mending service performed by volunteers is an economical solution to a constant need. This not only extends the useful life of the books, but also provides a savings that can result in more new acquisitions.

Volunteers might also assume much of the responsibility for the physical environment of the library or media center. Such tasks as controlling heat and ventilation, lighting and other simple tasks that contribute to the comfort of the learners are subtle, but positive contributions. Their efforts in arranging exhibits and displays and decorating can do much to foster an atmosphere of inquiry and stimulation.

VOLUNTEERS WORKING WITH CHILDREN IN THE LIBRARY

There are many ways that volunteers can be actively involved in working with children in a library. These efforts may include activities such as the following.

Story Hours

Studies have shown that children benefit in their language development if they are read to often. Volunteers can be used to conduct story hours on a regular basis. An informal setting where the youngsters sit on the floor and are read to for the expressed purpose of enjoying good literature may help to encourage better attitudes toward reading. The volunteers may need help in selecting materials appropriate to the age level. The library teacher or classroom teacher could prepare a list of suggested stories and poetry to be shared with the children. As the volunteers gain experience in reading to groups, they develop the proper sense of timing and voice emphasis that further enlivens the story time.

Story hours need not be confined to only the primary grades; upper grade children also enjoy hearing stories read aloud.

Book Discussion Groups

Volunteers may conduct discussion groups based on a book or story that each of the participating children has read. A small-group format is utilized to engage in a critique of a book selection. These groups may operate on a weekly basis and the students read a section of the book in preparation for each session. The role of the volunteer is to lead the discussion and to try to encourage each of the group members to contribute. With groups of gifted children, discussion might take place after the children have read the whole work. The depth of discussion and choice of materials is determined by the reading level of the participants. The volunteer would need the help of a professional in determining this information. You will want to be sure that those who lead such groups are fond of reading themselves. The primary purpose of such an activity is to promote the love of reading good works. Coercion, scolding, and excessive stress on minor details can prove to be contrary to this purpose. Since several copies of the same book are required, it may be wise to use paperback editions for this activity.

Helping Students with Research

Students working on projects are often in need of help to do the necessary research. Volunteers assigned to the reference area are available to assist the students in selecting the appropriate materials. They should be made familiar with the various resources and the proper use of each. The volunteer can also guide the students in the use of a card catalogue in finding various sources of information. The task of the volunteer is to help the student find the useful material, rather than actually making the selections.

Volunteers may also work with small groups in doing research. They can be helpful in assisting the students to coordinate the various elements of a group project. Young students sometimes need help when doing this kind of research so that they don't duplicate their individual efforts.

When volunteers are assigned to work with students engaged in research, you should impress upon them the fact that good research does not permit word-for-word copying from the source of information, except for instances where appropriate passages, properly quoted, are necessary. Students should be encouraged to take good notes and then to use these as a basis for writing a report. You will want to be sure that the paraprofessional is familiar with outlining procedures.

USING VOLUNTEERS TO OPERATE A SCHOOL LIBRARY

Many schools have a school library facility, but do not have sufficient funds to employ a professional librarian to operate it. In this situation, it is possible to run a very succesful library program using volunteers, with little or no cost. A very important factor in the success of such a program is to have a well-organized volunteer program that utilizes dependable people. The key person is, of course, the chairman of library volunteers who must be willing to spend the necessary time in recruiting and scheduling volunteers to work in the library.

A suggested list of duties and responsibilities for a school library chairman is as follows:

1. Help to recruit volunteers for the school library. This could be a cooperative effort between the school administration, teachers, and the chairman.
2. Establish a schedule of volunteers and provide the school and each volunteer with a copy.
3. Work with the school administration to schedule each of the classes for library use.
4. Keep school and volunteers informed of any changes in schedule. If change is permanent, update master schedule.

5. Assign substitutes where and when needed.
6. Bring any questions or problems to the attention of the teachers or school administration.
7. Help in the training and orientation of new volunteers.
8. Help to keep the morale and enthusiasm of the volunteers high.

In a library run by nonprofessionals, teachers must be urged to remain with their classes while they are using the library. The volunteers are there only to assist in the operation of the library. The nature of their employment is such that they should not be made responsible for a group of children.

Dear Parents,

We are in need of volunteers to assist in the library. This is an opportunity for you to be helpful to the school program and to enjoy the benefits of working with children.

No special skills are required to be a library volunteer. The major task is to help in the circulation procedures and this is an activity that is easily learned.

Some volunteers will also be trained as book menders. Other helpful activities are helping students do research and updating the card catalogue.

If you have some time (an hour per week is enough) and would like to become involved in helping the school, please contact me at the number listed below.

We hope to hear from you soon.

Yours truly,

Mary Smith
Chairman of Library Volunteers
327-0081

**LETTER FROM CHAIRMAN OF
LIBRARY VOLUNTEERS TO PARENTS**

Duty	Time	Monday	Tuesday	Wednesday	Thursday	Friday
Assist Librarian	9:00 11:00	Mrs. Jones	Mrs. Brown	Mrs. Gray	Mrs. Smith	Mrs. Harris
Book Repair	9:00 11:00		Mrs. Riley and Mrs. Scott		Mrs. Keane and Mrs. Paul	
Assist Librarian	12:00 2:00	Mrs. Black	Mrs. West	Mrs. White	Mrs. Campbell	Mrs. James
Book Repair	12:00 2:00			Mrs. Starr and Mrs. Lane		

BLOCK SCHEDULE FOR LIBRARY VOLUNTEERS

A suggested list of responsibilities and duties for library volunteers is as follows:

1. Assist the teacher by helping the students check books in and out.
2. Keep the shelves properly arranged and in good order.
3. Be prompt and dependable in attendance. If it is necessary to be absent, inform the chairman of volunteers.
4. Take care of the physical condition of the library — heating, ventilation, lighting, and general appearance.
5. Always check in and out at the school office. Be alert for any notices pertaining to the library.
6. Discuss any questions or problems with the chairman or school personnel.
7. Teachers will accompany students to the library. Refer discipline problems to them.
8. Small groups or individuals are permitted to use the library. The volunteer need not tolerate misbehavior, but should refer problems to the classroom teacher.

If this type of operation is to succeed, you must provide the volunteer with proper training and orientation to the school facility. This may be accomplished by using the techniques described in an earlier chapter. A handbook for library volunteers is also a useful item.

TEACHER AIDES ASSISTING IN THE LIBRARY

You may, of course, use a teacher aide in any of the capacities described previously for volunteers. Since an aide is a paid employee and is available on a more regular basis, you may find more ways to utilize their services.

Using an Aide to Assist a Teacher-Librarian

An aide can be of great assistance to a professional librarian. By assuming the major responsibility for the circulation of books, the aide frees the librarian to work with students. The aide may also keep the card files and the shelves in order as a part of her daily routine.

You may use an aide to set up a resource shelf after the librarian has made selections. Aides may also be given the responsibility for assisting in the repair of books. An aide, as a paraprofessional, may be helpful in a number of ways in a clerical or tutorial capacity. The major responsibility of the teacher-librarian will then be to develop library skills in students as well as teachers.

Using Aides When a Professional Librarian Is Not Available

Teacher aides may be employed to help operate a library when there is no regular teacher-librarian. A teacher aide working in this capacity helps to coordinate the activities of the volunteers and provides better continuity to the library program than would be possible with a set of volunteers. The major responsibility of the aide is to ensure that the library is available and that the collection is kept in good order so that it may be of use to the students and teachers.

In this arrangement the classroom teacher should remain with the class when the whole class uses the library. The teacher should assume the major responsibility for the group while in the library. The aide may help individuals or may assist in the checking in and out of books.

Story hours and discussion groups may also be supervised by the aide with the cooperation of the classroom teacher.

A suggested list of duties and responsibilities for a teacher's aide-librarian is as follows:

1. Be sure that the library is in good order.
2. Take charge of the circulation procedures with respect to each group that uses the library.
3. Help train volunteers in their roles as library helpers.
4. Schedule the volunteers for their library work periods.

5. Discuss library problems and needs with the school administrator.
6. Assist teacher in setting up reserve shelves.
7. Assist students in doing research.
8. Find substitute volunteers when necessary.
9. Report overdue books to respective classroom teachers.
10. Help to encourage use of the library by maintaining an efficient, pleasant atmosphere.

USING VOLUNTEERS AND AIDES IN MEDIA CENTERS

Operating a successful media center could be more readily assured if a number of well trained aides and/or volunteers are available to assist the resource teacher. Since a media center has, in addition to printed materials, a vast array of audio-visual software and hardware, it becomes a more complex operation than a traditional library. The task of keeping track of all of this equipment and seeing that it is properly used and maintained becomes almost too much for one person. Properly trained aides and volunteers can assume many responsibilities that are time consuming, yet essential to the successful operation of a media center.

AIDES AND VOLUNTEERS AS RESEARCH ASSISTANTS

Students using a media center need much help in locating material and in using the media equipment that is available. You may assign aides or volunteers to assist them. Such items as filmstrips, tapes, films, film loops, records, slides, and video tape recordings all require fairly sophisticated media devices for their utilization. They all must be filed in a logical way and recorded in a central filing system. Students and teachers need to become familiar with this system and require the help of aides or volunteers in the proper retrieval of this information.

The volunteer-aide may work with individuals on specific projects or may work with small groups. If enough volunteers are available, they may be given specific responsibilities for certain types of equipment. For example, one volunteer may be in charge of the filmstrips and the filmstrip previewer. If a student needs to use this medium, he would seek the assistance of this volunteer. The persons assigned to these various learning areas would keep the resource teacher informed as to the condition of the software and hardware and provide information regarding specific needs.

A sample list of duties for people working in special areas is as follows:

1. Assist students and teachers in doing research.
2. Maintain the filing system for the media software in this area.
3. Keep an inventory of the hardware and report shortages to the resource teacher.
4. Make note of items in need of repair and refer to them to the person responsible.
5. Keep records of the utilization of specific items. This information is useful in reordering.

USING VOLUNTEERS AND AIDES IN THE REPAIR AND MAINTENANCE OF EQUIPMENT

A major problem in the operation of a media center is keeping the media software and hardware in a good state of repair.

Routine maintenance can easily be performed by trained aides or volunteers. Torn or broken filmstrips, tapes, and films can be spliced and used again. The procedure for splicing is simple and easily learned by volunteers or aides. You may choose to make this the major responsibility of a group of helpers. If the repair equipment is available, a number of tasks can be taken care of in the media center itself.

Some of these are:

1. Splicing of tapes, films, filmstrips, video tapes.
2. Copying tapes, video tapes, and slides.
3. Editing films and tapes.

Equipment such as tape recorders, filmstrip projectors, film projectors, phonographs, previewers, and others require routine preventive maintenance to keep them functioning properly. A maintenance checklist for each piece of equipment should be developed. Aides or volunteers could be assigned to perform this maintenance. A sample checklist is included in this chapter.

It should not be assumed that volunteer help can perform major repairs. What is referred to here are such things as bulb replacement, oiling, replacing belts, superficial cleaning of lenses and surface areas, and similar duties. Major repairs must be done by a skilled technician. Volunteers and aides who are familiar with the equipment and aware of a malfunction may be able to prevent further damage by removing the equipment from use and referring it for repairs.

Equipment: Ampro Movie Projector 16 mm
Model: JT 11
Serial Number: 87214
Inventory Number: K 821
Bulb: OH 2

Hours Used

Date	3/11/72		
Number of hrs.	1 hr.		
Oiled			
Date	2/25/72		
Bulb Replaced			
Date	3/1/72		
Lens Cleaned			
Date	2/27/72		

Comments:

MAINTENANCE AND USE CHECKLIST

We have seen how volunteers can be used in libraries and media centers to perform a variety of tasks. School libraries may be operated solely by volunteers if a trained librarian is not available.

The most important function for library or media volunteers is to assist the professional in providing the best opportunities for learning for all students. This assistance includes working with students as well as clerical and housekeeping chores that help to extend the effectiveness of the library or media center.

Volunteers and Teacher Aides in Early Childhood Education / 4

The use of volunteers and teacher aides on the prekindergarten and kindergarten levels is of great importance for many reasons. Not only are children between the ages of three and six much less self-reliant than older children, they are able to learn more during these years than at any other similar time period in their school careers. Current educational and behavioral research indicates that more knowledge, attitude development, and emotional pattern setting takes place during these early years than was commonly believed by even the most enlightened educators during past generations. The creative use of auxiliary personnel in the classroom can result in meaningful growth in children that will help them in their efforts throughout their later years in school. Therefore, it is vital that those who assist you in your work with preschool-aged children be appropriately suited to the task. This work should not be taken lightly. As more and more educational leaders come to realize that kindergarten and prekindergarten experiences are very significant for children, so must we plan to make the contributions by those who work with our young children meaningful and productive.

VOLUNTEERS IN PREPRIMARY PROGRAMS

Preprimary classes vary greatly in scope and function from private babysitting nursery schools to sophisticated prekindergarten public school programs. Thousands of American children are in state and Federally funded programs like Head Start, which attempt to provide extra help to those who are penalized unnecessarily by poverty and other forms of deprivation. In this chapter we will concentrate on the basic principles and methods that are common to all good preprimary programs, as well as provide a brief focus on programs for those in poverty areas.

VOLUNTEERS IN HEAD START PROGRAMS

In regard to volunteers in Head Start and other programs that deal with many problems relating to the economically or culturally deprived, special emphasis must be placed on those human factors that tend to be more prevalent in poverty areas. The scarcity of sufficient family income often puts the poor child at a disadvantage regarding material things such as toys, books, records, and travel, all of which provide natural stimulation for learning through vocabulary development and varied experiences. This child is also at a disadvantage because the level of education of his parents is most often less than that of high school completion. An inadequate diet may also be an obstacle to academic achievement for many children.

Volunteers who work in programs for children with some of these handicaps must be truly sensitive to and aware of the needs of the children with whom they come in contact. They must be people who can readily accept the fact that life styles other than those of the middle class exist in our society.

The need to show affection, understanding, and constancy is most important with children of all ages. Poor children often have extra needs that may result from the absence of one or both parents, or an overworked parent who is unable to devote the proper amount of time to family needs. Volunteers must be able to give generously of more than just their time. They must demonstrate warmth and patience. For this reason you will want to be certain that the volunteer is a reasonably well-adjusted person who is free of moodiness, sarcasm, and a short temper. The careful selection of volunteers for this level can not be ignored.

ACTIVITIES FOR VOLUNTEERS IN PREPRIMARY PROGRAMS

The kinds of activities that can be performed by volunteers in preprimary programs are many and varied. They are determined by the skills and abilities of the volunteers and by the needs of the children involved. The services they perform are of immense value, but care must be taken that those who set budgets and allocate funds do not see the use of part-time volunteers as a means of eliminating teacher aides from early childhood programs. There can be no reasonable substitute for the continuity provided by your well-trained aides. Of the multitude of possible activities, listed here are some of major significance.

Clothing

The simple task of supervising dressing and undressing by aides provides valuable time for the teacher to perform other tasks. Teachers should encourage volunteers to help the young children as much as possible to become more self-reliant. The adults' dressing and undressing children in order to save time can ultimately result in more time loss because the children will take longer to learn to care for themselves. The volunteers should help children to hang their clothes in the appropriate place and put boots and rubbers where they belong. They should not be overly concerned when children take a long time to remove snowpants and other garments. Unless the child experiences real frustration, he will gain valuable skills by working at this task as much as possible.

One-to-One Relationship

Being a good listener helps in the development of young children. Again, the volunteer must be encouraged to let the children engage in the activity as much as possible. For example, if the volunteer is examining a book with a child, the volunteer should encourage the child to explain the picture rather than explaining the picture to the child. When the child exhibits a reluctance to speak, the volunteer might attempt to engage him through simple questions such as: "What does *your* baby sister do?" "Is your street like the one in the picture?" "What does it look like?"

When correcting children, volunteers should use the positive approach. Rather than saying, "Don't throw the puzzle pieces," say, "The pieces belong on this table." Instead of, "Don't stand on the swing," they might say, "Sit on the swing." They should not cause the child to feel inferior by saying things like, "You're a big boy now, you shouldn't act like a baby." Statements like these, even when said calmly and sweetly, are often counter-productive.

Volunteers should be trained to work at the children's physical level by squatting or sitting on a low chair so that the child can see the volunteer's face. They must be sure that the child knows the adult is listening when the child talks. When the adult answers the child his voice and facial expression should be friendly and pleasant. When answering questions the volunteer should avoid talking too much. The child may not be interested in or able to assimilate more than a simple and brief answer.

The volunteer should never make fun of a child or compare him with another child by making statements like: "Johnny has put *his* puzzle where it belongs." The adult must also make every attempt to be honest. If there is insufficient time to play a particular game, the adult should not say, "Perhaps we can play that later." The volunteer should avoid discussing a child in his presence even if the child seems to be occupied with an activity at the time and does not appear to be listening.

Outdoor Activities

Volunteers who help with outdoor playground and other activities must be made aware of the importance of safety. If asked by the teacher or trained aide to supervise a particular piece of play equipment, it is important that they know the necessary safety rules associated with the apparatus and that they give serious attention to it. For example, if children are asked to descend on slides feet first only, it is important that the children observe the rule consistently to avoid accidents.

It is not unusual for the staff members to forget that volunteers, who help for as little as one or two hours each week, may not know the safety rules, especially when a class uses several volunteers each week. For this reason it is advisable to duplicate a simple list of the safety rules so that each volunteer can study them before assuming supervisory duties.

Housekeeping

There are virtually scores of ways in which volunteers can assist the teacher with housekeeping chores. Picking up after art and play activities is one that always exists in early childhood programs. Stress to the volunteers that they are helping the children to pick up; the children are not helping them. The act of putting things away in proper order is important to children, as important as the activity itself in many instances. The volunteer can help by guiding and encouraging. Sometimes it helps to make a game of picking up. Subtle instruction also takes place when the adult says: "Let's pick up all the blue blocks first," "Let's take two at a time," "Long ones first, then short ones."

During painting time volunteers can assist with aprons, helping children to wipe spills, hanging wet pictures, and marking the child's name on the back of his work. The volunteer should be encouraged to print the child's name clearly, another learning opportunity for children.

Art Expression

It is important that volunteers learn that the ways in which a child expresses himself at the easel, with clay, blocks, rhythms, and other means are unique to him and must come from him. It is not necessary for his work to look realistic.

The adult should not "teach" the preschool child to make real objects. The volunteer should also encourage and praise the child for his creative work and avoid comparing his work with that of other children.

In each early childhood program there are many ways in which children develop through self-expression. They may paste; cut with scissors; use crayons, clay, blocks, and tools; paint; play at doll corners; have water play; as well as engage in many other activities. For each activity the teacher has specific procedures to follow in even the most free and informal classroom or center. Care must be taken to train volunteers in the basic procedures for the activities with which they assist in order to insure reasonable efficiency. The time taken by the teacher or trained aide to do this will result in manifold gains and prove to be an ultimate time saver because there will be less need for repeated re-teaching as the year progresses.

Enrichment

Volunteers bring to the classroom a multitude of skills, talents, and experience backgrounds. The creative principal, supervisor, and teacher will take advantage of this by putting these attributes to good use. You might have among your volunteer group such people as former teachers, secretaries, artists, and travelers — all with special contributions to make, which even the most resourceful teacher might not be able to bring to her classroom.

Volunteers who bring interesting objects to the classroom from time to time provide an excellent service. These objects might include such items as foreign dolls and costumes, special toys, games, books, tools, and many others.

Some volunteers may have special talents for dramatic play. They can read or tell a story in such ways that children become enthralled with the activity. This is an excellent way to increase the child's vocabulary and develop his ability to express himself while building in him a love for the written and spoken word. Again, it might be wise to stress here that active involvement by the children is important. Be careful that the volunteer does not dominate the stage exclusively. Much value comes from activities in which children act out with others stories and incidents from real or imaginary life situations. The volunteer might be the visitor who comes to dinner, or the audience for a puppet show, circus, or other shows.

Volunteers can assist outside of the classroom as well as in it. In programs that deal with children from families with limited incomes, there is frequently a need to transport mothers to the school for conferences or special activities. On occasion children need to be taken to clinics, doctors, or dentists. Volunteers have been extremely helpful in arranging for medical personnel to contribute services at the school, hospital, or medical office. Their personal acquaintances with various resource people in the community can sometimes bring benefits to the program which would have been nearly impossible without their help.

You must not rely only on the volunteer orientation and early training programs to insure success of volunteers with young children. In addition to at least one careful interview, most schools ask for and investigate references that prospective volunteers are asked to furnish. A volunteer who is not appropriately suited to work with very young children can often be effective in other kinds of school volunteer work in the upper grades. There is also a place for volunteers outside of the classroom doing clerical work, publicity, and other tasks.

TEACHER AIDES IN PREPRIMARY PROGRAMS

No volunteer program can replace the intelligent and efficient use of trained full-time teacher aides. Aides provide the daily assistance and reinforcement so vital to the development of the very young child. For this reason great care must be taken to select the best people. College training is not always an indication that a prospective aide will be suitable for working with children in early childhood programs. They must give evidence of having affection and concern for children. Adults who are reasonably even-tempered and patient will find working with young children more gratifying than will those who do not possess these qualities.

Most of the activities outlined above for volunteers are activities in which teacher aides take part. As an important part of the team of principal-supervisor, teacher and volunteers, aides can play a major role in planning programs for the children as well. As aides become proficient in the regular routine and sensitive to the needs of individual children, they can be of help to the professional staff in determining what activities will best fit into the child's development.

It is important to stress here that early childhood programs where teacher aides are employed use aides in different ways and give them varying degrees of responsibility. Some Head Start programs employ paraprofessionals in teaching capacities. This practice is best avoided if budgets will permit the employment of properly certified teachers. That is not to say, however, that aides should not be given more responsibility as they prove worthy. It is often advisable to have levels of early childhood paraprofessionals who might be called "aides," "assistant teachers," "deputy teachers," or any of several designations. Having varying classifications with differentiated levels of responsibility and salary will also provide them with an excellent incentive to improve their status. Encouraging paraprofessionals to acquire appropriate college credits is also advisable. Some boards of education or other funding agencies arrange either tuition payments or special courses and workshops through teacher training institutions at no cost to the participants who are employed by the schools.

When aide programs that rely upon carefully planned preschool and in-service training are compared with those that do not, the value of training becomes very apparent. You may find yourself in the position of having to employ and assign aides within a short period of time because of factors like finding a funding source not previously expected, or having to meet deadlines imposed by negotiated provisions in the teacher-board of education contract agreement. When this occurs, it would be advisable to resist rushing in favor of careful recruiting and well-planned training programs geared to meeting the specific needs of the schools.

In addition to the activities already mentioned above for volunteers, which are also within the scope of teacher aides' duties, we list here some points that are pertinent to early childhood teacher-aide programs.

TEACHER-AIDE SUPERVISION OF CHILDREN

It is important that teacher aides look upon their role in supervising children in a positive light. They might see themselves as partners rather than directors; as facilitators of learning rather than teachers. They must realize that children differ greatly in size, temperament, color, behavior, maturity, and interest. All, however, need love and understanding. Children who seem least lovable are probably in need of greater love and understanding. Children are sensitive to the actions of others. A seemingly innocent remark can cause children to feel insecure or fearful. A friendly relationship between the aide and the child based on sympathy, affection, tolerance, and a sense of humor is the best guard against the negative forces that can and sometimes do exist in the classroom.

When supervising young children, the teacher aide must be guided by the knowledge that young children develop best when they possess confidence and a good self-image as well as esteem for others. Those character attributes are best developed when adults guide and encourage rather than command and scold.

To establish the proper relationship, it helps if the aide learns and uses the names of the children as soon as possible. Taking time to have friendly talks with the children and showing them that they, the volunteers, have a genuine interest in the children's general progress and needs should be an important part of the aide's work. Sometimes new aides will think they demonstrate their eagerness and overall worth best by "keeping busy." They must realize that they are working when they take time to relate to the children with warmth and sincere interest. If a paint spill or an overturned crayon box is allowed to stand an extra few minutes, or the doll corner becomes disarranged while the aide is engaged in a meaningful conversation, or while she is helping a child to discover a concept, she shouldn't feel guilty. An orderly room does not necessarily result in a good program. The best early childhood programs help to stimulate curiosity and discovery in children which will, in turn, result in self-motivation for problem solving.

EXPANDED ACTIVITIES WITH TEACHER AIDES

Even those preschool or kindergarten teachers who were most reluctant to have aides in their classroom wonder how they ever managed without them after they work with an effective aide for a few months. One reason for this is that the variety of meaningful activities teachers can bring to their classrooms can now be broadened. More interest centers and exhibits can be established and maintained with an extra pair of hands. Water play, carpentry, crafts, dramatic play, storytelling, reading and reading readiness, field trips, more parent conferences, science experiments, and many other activities can be introduced or increased.

One of the most significant benefits comes from the increased time that will now be available to the teacher to provide for more individual attention to children and to communicate with parents and other resource people.

The benefits which come from using volunteers and teacher aides in preprimary programs are many. But before embarking on volunteer or teacher-aide programs, various factors must be considered to ensure success. Adults who plan to work with very young children must be warm, sympathetic, and understanding of the many differences that exist in children physically, emotionally, intellectually, and culturally.

After you have selected the best people, they should be exposed to a suitable training program that is based on developing an understanding of the growth and development of very young children, as well as the components of early childhood programs.

With careful selection and training, volunteers and teacher aides provide valuable services in housekeeping, clerical work, supervision, and instruction, as well as curriculum enrichment through discovery for problem solving. The activities that can be offered can now be broadened to include many creative and meaningful experiences for the three-to-six-year-old that meet his individual needs and provide better opportunities for his growth and development.

Volunteers and Aides in the Primary Classroom

5

Children in the initial phases of skill development require much individual attention. Many are still in need of help in performing personal tasks such as putting on or removing outer garments and boots. The teacher often finds it difficult at dismissal time to help everyone get ready to board the school buses. Consequently, time has to be taken from instruction to accomplish these tasks. These chores and many others can easily be assumed by the paraprofessional. This chapter will present many ways primary teachers can utilize aides or volunteers to improve their effectiveness. While the teacher provides most of the professional planning and preparation, the volunteer-aides are the extra pairs of hands, ears, and eyes that extend the teacher's ability to meet the needs of all.

PROVIDING FOR INDIVIDUALIZED INSTRUCTION

Many people erroneously think that an individualized program means that each child must be given a set of tasks that are unique and tailor-made for him. In every class there are many children with similar specific needs. For example, ten out of twenty-five children in a first grade class may be experiencing difficulty in hearing consonants, five might not know the colors, and seven might be ready to read the first reader. The combinations of ability groups are interchangeable and endless.

A multitude of simple testing procedures together with teacher judgment help to identify and formulate these groups. Using one or more aides or volunteers to present or monitor progress, specific work is prepared for each group or individual. It might appear to be an awesome task for the teacher who is responsible for the entire class. However, it must be remembered that as paraprofessionals become aware of the needs of the group or individual child and the methods used to help them, she can do more and more of the work with a minimum of supervision from the teacher. Outlined below are only a few of the kinds of activities that can be conducted by the paraprofessional.

Worksheets and Workbooks

The assistance of paraprofessionals frees the teacher from the concern for finding a single spirit duplicated or other prepared material to meet the needs of her class. She may now use many different kinds of materials to meet individual needs. As the aides or volunteers become familiar with these materials, they can assume a greater share of the responsibility for correcting the work done by the children, assisting them with it as it is being done, and select or prepare the next task that takes the child to the next step in his skill development or understanding.

When children receive additional supervision and individualized help, whether individually or in small groups, their productivity increases substantially. Without assistance, even the most competent and efficient teacher experiences frustration in providing suitable work for each child. As the level and amount of work are established, the children as well as the teacher are able to function more comfortably. The child who becomes bored because he finishes early will now have tasks that provide more challenge. The slower child will not be as ready to engage in antisocial behavior out of frustration with his work, but will be able to get the required assistance to experience success.

As the paraprofessional gains skill and understanding, you may, with less concern, assign the task of preparing worksheets and other materials to her. A degree of monitoring by the professional staff will always be necessary, however, to insure proper growth of the child. The physical task of running duplicating machines and preparing material for duplication can easily be assumed by the paraprofessional after a minimum of training.

BETTER READING AND LANGUAGE ARTS INSTRUCTION

Among the most important activities that take place in primary classrooms are those that are concerned with language arts and reading. Success in this area helps to determine success in almost every subject to which children are exposed throughout their school years. There are many activities with which teacher aides or parent volunteers can be of great service. Discussed below are only some of the many methods that are of value and can be conducted without requiring an excessive amount of time and energy from the teacher or supervisor.

Listening to Children Read

This simple activity is of great help to children. When one considers the number of children in the average primary classroom and the many responsibilities of the teacher, it becomes obvious that the amount of time spent listening to children read is often inadequate. Those who assist the teacher can be of immeasurable help here without the need for extensive training.

It is important to stress to the teacher aides, parent volunteers, or student volunteers who engage in this activity that patience is of paramount importance. Unless planned by the teacher, sophisticated instructional methods need not be employed. The paraprofessional need only listen and calmly supply the words the child misses. The practice of supplying words should continue as long as the child shows need. The child should not detect a note of exasperation or impatience in the listener. Praise for the successes of the child should be encouraged and overreaction to error or mispronunciation always discouraged. The volunteer or aide must display an interest in the child's effort.

This activity is of great value to the child because it provides for reinforcement of his reading skills. It also is helpful in the improvement of pronunciation and as a means of acquiring new sight words.

Reading to Children

Volunteers and teacher aides can also be of great help here in many ways. The teacher can devote much-needed time to individuals and small groups while the paraprofessional conducts this useful activity with others. This is an activity that is very popular among parent volunteers for it can be done at times that suit their schedules. It must be stressed that participation in this activity should not be taken lightly. Hearing stories read well helps children to develop an interest in reading, builds their vocabulary, and gives pleasure. Those who engage in this activity should become familiar with the material and practice their delivery. With practice, the paraprofessional can become quite talented at this task and gain personal satisfaction as she develops her "theatrical" skills. It is wise to check on her performance before she begins this activity.

Scribble Stories

A very helpful exercise for the volunteers and aides is in the preparation of scribble stories with the young learner. The student, who is a nonwriter or beginner, dictates the story and makes his scribble marks to indicate his meaning. He then repeats the story to the one who is helping him. The person then transcribes the scribble marks into words using manuscript rather than cursive writing.

The completed text may be used by the teacher for a reading lesson using the student's own vocabulary as a basis for his learning to read. This activity not only enables the student to express himself in writing, it also gives him the satisfaction of playing a key role in the development of his own reading skills. The function of the volunteer helper is to faithfully interpret students' scribble into words without changing his meaning. The stories can be saved and later bound in simple fashion to form booklets that may be used to build a classroom library comprised of contributions from each child.

Experience Stories

The experience story is a valid learning device and one in which the volunteer or aide may prove helpful in many ways. Students may dictate narratives based on some incident or other personal experience in their lives. The adult (or older student) acts as a recorder and puts the story into words. The student then may illustrate the story and put it in the form of a book. This may be used much the same as a scribble story as learning material in the reading process. If a primary typewriter is available to type the story, it puts the text in a more readable form and one that resembles a regular reading book.

Other Language Arts Activities

There are many other ways in which paraprofessionals can be of service to the primary reading and language arts program. They might keep records and charts of books read by children in individualized reading programs. Assisting children in the selection of materials and discussing what the children have read are helpful practices. Working with small groups on specific phonics skills, using flashcards for word recognition and vocabulary development, are activities that can also be effectively conducted by aides and volunteers.

MATH SKILL DEVELOPMENT

In addition to the valuable reading and language arts instructional tasks performed by paraprofessionals, they may also provide valuable service in the math program. There are many useful activities that are most helpful, yet do not require a math background on the part of the volunteer or aide.

Concept Development

When new concepts are introduced to a class, rarely do all of the children exhibit the same degree of understanding. Some comprehend immediately, others will need further explanation and reinforcement. As these children are identified, they may be put into groups of varying sizes for different needs. In this situation the teacher profits greatly from assistants. Individual help may be given immediately, rather than having the very bright and the slower children wait for their turns. Frequently, it is helpful for the volunteer or aide to hear the teacher's initial presentation so that her method, terminology, and materials will allow for a smooth and sequential development as the teacher introduces new concepts and procedures. The aide must generally use the same techniques as the teacher when teaching concepts. New methods differ substantially from those of the past. When working with aides or volunteers, it is important that you stress the prescribed math methodology that usually allows for sufficient flexibility in presentation.

Reinforcing Skills

Teachers know that a successful math program relies on skill development based on the understanding of concepts. Since the skill development will differ among the children, the aides and volunteers can work with individuals and small groups. The aide's ability to monitor and correct work while it is being done by the children is of utmost importance. The child will not develop incorrect procedures that have to be unlearned. With the assistance of other pairs of hands, the teacher can correct papers immediately rather than after school. The immediacy this provides is much more beneficial to the children who may forget much of what they attempted to do the previous day.

Manipulative Materials and Games

Activities using manipulative materials and games have long been recognized as useful ways for young children to

develop an understanding of concepts. With the paraprofessionals assisting the teacher, they can be conducted effectively. Available today are many suitable materials at reasonable costs. Better still, paraprofessionals can assist children
to make or develop their own materials and games. The
possibilities are endless and the materials can be almost
anything — spools, milk cartons, straws, boxes, buttons,
sticks, beads, or plastic containers. These materials can be
used to develop sets and other modern math concepts.

Flashcards are a particularly useful activity for paraprofessionals since they are simple to use and require little
monitoring on the part of the teacher. Sets of cards that are
appropriate to specific ability levels can be used with much
benefit in skill reinforcement.

PREPARATION OF MATERIALS

Much has already been said about aides and volunteers
assisting in the preparation of materials used for individualized learning. It must be remembered that while these people
can effectively take charge of duplicating and preparing
simple materials, the preparation of specific material used as
a prescription for correcting learning deficiencies in children
must be carefully supervised by the professional staff. Well-
trained paraprofessionals frequently can and do become
proficient at this with a minimum of monitoring by the teacher
or supervisor. Sound professional judgment and the nature
of the content or remediation will determine the extent to
which paraprofessionals may assume more responsibilities.
The kinds of materials that can be prepared by paraprofessionals are many.

Overhead Transparencies and Spirit Masters

These are common materials that can be prepared
with little advanced training. As the volunteers or teacher
aides become skillful at this, the teacher needs merely to
select the appropriate material to be typed, duplicated, col-
lated, or in some way prepared. One aide or volunteer who
is effective in the mechanical process of preparing materials
can be used to train others, thus freeing you from this task.

Room Decoration and Bulletin Boards

It is not unusual to find classrooms that were formerly drab and uninteresting suddenly sparkle with creative bulletin boards and colorful displays after aides or parent volunteers were introduced. Even hard-working teachers are often guilty of having unattractive classrooms because of the lack of time or real or imagined inability to be artistic. Often paraprofessionals who lack confidence before a group of children display excellent skills in room decoration, lettering, bulletin board display, and exhibit tables. Children tend to enjoy school more when their classrooms provide interesting and stimulating things to study and observe. With help, the teacher need no longer leave the seasonal display beyond the point where it ceases to hold interest.

A word of caution to those who are fortunate enough to have the assistance of talented aides or volunteers: Whenever possible, children's work should be featured in displays and bulletin boards. Even the most artistic should not substitute their work for the children's. The way the children's work is displayed and the way children are taught to display their work can be greatly improved with the guidance of adults who have talents in this area.

CREATING INTEREST CENTERS

As modern schools progress in an effort to individualize children's learning, the concept of interest centers in primary classrooms comes into prominence. In the open classroom concept, which has met with much interest and acceptance, interest centers are of great importance. With tables, counters, or sections of classrooms designated for special subjects, projects, or hobbies, additional pairs of hands are essential. Indeed, the effective use of active interest centers in a primary classroom is close to impossible when the teacher conducts her class without adult aid. The ways in which this assistance can be rendered are numerous. Outlined here are some of the kinds of interest centers and tasks which can be accomplished by aides and volunteers:

Science
1. Gathering materials, specimens, etc.
2. Setting up displays
3. Developing and illustrating charts
4. Demonstrating
5. Conducting and assisting with simple experiments under the direction of the teacher
6. Organizing and labeling collections
7. Caring for pets and other animals

Social Studies
1. Gathering pictures and other materials
2. Helping children to make displays, models, dioramas, etc.
3. Developing charts and maps with children
4. Constructing miniature scenes
5. Demonstrating
6. Teaching ethnic songs and dances

Math
1. Displaying concrete visuals to foster arithmetic concepts
2. Developing simple manipulative devices and games
3. Using homemade materials
4. Using balance scales
5. Preparing graphs and charts
6. Measuring objects found in the classroom
7. Taping record drill procedures for computational skills

Art
1. Putting out materials
2. Helping with materials
3. Cleaning up
4. Helping to display and demonstrate
5. Monitoring projects

Corner Store
1. Bringing in empty store items
2. Arranging and displaying items

3. Conducting "sales" and "purchases"
4. Making out orders for supplies

Sewing and Cooking Corner
1. Teaching skills
2. Collecting material
3. Displaying work
4. Cleaning up

ASSISTING IN CLASSROOM ROUTINE

The responsibilities of primary grade teachers that go beyond teaching are numerous. In addition to taking attendance and lunch counts, there are many records and reports to complete. Needless to say, many of these tasks can be assumed by the paraprofessional.

Other clerical tasks that can be done effectively by paraprofessionals is the correcting of children's work and recording of marks. This service provides the teacher with an excellent opportunity to devote time to other professional matters. It is important, however, that the teacher keep sufficiently abreast of individual children's progress so that proper materials can be prescribed for them. With this in mind, it is sometimes beneficial for the teacher to alternate sets of papers for correction so that she is aware of short-term progress; teachers must be careful not to turn too much of this responsibility over to the aide.

When using the services of volunteers for record keeping, it should be remembered that some information should not be made available to them. This information includes reports that bear upon the child's health and the health of his parents if the parents do not wish to have the information readily available to unauthorized personnel. It also includes reports concerning psychological evaluations of the child or members of his family. Often reports include information that pertains to former marriages of parents, adoptions, foster parents, and so on. Obviously, this should not be available to volunteers without parental permission.

Many teachers find that with assistance they are able to maintain up-to-date subject and picture files. Volunteers and aides with business experience often develop efficient classroom filing systems that increase the efficiency and productivity of the teacher.

The task of handing out notices for parents at the end of the day, while a simple chore, can be done effectively by the paraprofessional without taking away from the teacher's professional endeavors in the classroom. The matter of getting young children ready for recess, lunch, and dismissal no longer need consume valuable teaching time when the adults assist. With very young children, the teacher often must assist children with boots and coats. Surely a bachelor's degree is not a requirement for this task.

SUPERVISING PLAYGROUNDS AND LUNCHROOMS

In some localities the supervision of children during lunch or at play cannot be assumed by noncertified school personnel. Where this is not the case, they can be utilized to assist in this capacity and be of immeasurable help to the teacher. Much learning takes place during these times in the school day. With extra pairs of hands, ears, and eyes, the children can be taught better table manners and sportsmanship. This is helpful in reducing the number of accidents and instances of antisocial behavior.

Where permitted, all or part of the supervision for lunchrooms, playgrounds, and buses can be assumed by paraprofessionals. When this is done, the importance of training must be stressed. Some paraprofessionals tend to conduct these activities with ease, others experience difficulties. Young children need to feel a sense of confidence and consistency in the one who is supervising. Unless the procedures and rules are reasonably constant, these activities can become disruptive and frustrating for all. For this reason, regularly employed aides or volunteers who help on a daily basis must be carefully prepared for a supervisory assignment.

WORKING WITH LEARNING DISABILITIES

Much has been written of late about children with learning disabilities. Sometimes they are called children with perceptual handicaps or dyslexia. The educational prescriptions for such children are many and varied. In most cases it is difficult for the teacher who works alone to find the time to do all that is required. The teacher aides or volunteers can be used for these time-consuming and individualized activities. The ways in which they can perform these services vary with differing approaches. Following are some:

1. Practicing writing on the chalkboard.
2. Catching and throwing a ball or a beanbag.
3. Walking on a balance beam or other similar device.
4. Monitoring workbook activities which are designed to assist in the remediation of a perceptual problem.

CONCLUSION

We have attempted to outline some approaches for using aides in primary classrooms. Even if only a few of the ideas are employed, the introduction of aides and volunteers to the classroom provides an immense service to teachers and young children. The aides and volunteers assist with the much-needed emphasis on individualized learning by being the extra pairs of hands, ears, and eyes so necessary in the modern classroom. They monitor the efforts of children who need special help in reading, math, and other subjects. They provide invaluable assistance with the many burdensome tasks related to record keeping, classroom routine, playground and lunchroom supervision, as well as to enrich the classroom with creative displays, bulletin boards, and interest centers. Their assistance in the vital area of primary grade reading and language arts alone more than justifies their existence, which becomes more imperative each year.

Using Volunteers and Teacher Aides in Intermediate Grades and Secondary Schools

6

Volunteers and aides may be used in the intermediate and upper grades as effectively as they are in the primary grades. Many of the activities that are carried on are similar at all levels of instruction. Youngsters with reading problems are found at all levels, as are those with deficiencies in other skill areas. Enrichment programs in the basic skills and in the arts can be augmented by the use of aides and/or volunteers.

Volunteers with expertise in certain fields can be called upon to lead special-interest groups and to form clubs that meet during and after school hours. Volunteers can assist teachers in preparing materials and in the clerical responsibilities that are part of instruction.

Often in recruiting volunteers to work with older children, it is necessary to reassure them that they are not expected to be experts in the skills with which they will help the students. They should be assured that they will be given the necessary guidance to enable them to adequately help the students. Much of what they will do does not require the technical knowledge of a teacher. Their primary role is to assist the students and give them the confidence and reassurance they need to learn successfully.

INDIVIDUAL INSTRUCTION WITH THE
HELP OF AIDES AND VOLUNTEERS

The key factors in individualizing instruction are careful diagnosis of the students' needs and effective planning to help satisfy these needs. Most of the responsibility for the accomplishment of these tasks rests with the teachers and the school administration. Volunteer-aides may be helpful in assisting the teachers by administering some of the diagnostic materials and helping in the compilation of data to be used in the planning for the course of action to be taken.

When the plan of instruction for an individual or a group of students is determined, the teacher should discuss with the volunteer the role she is to play in its implementation.

Individualized instruction necessitates the use of a variety of materials, some commercially prepared and some teacher-prepared. The volunteer, with brief instruction, may assume some of the responsibility for the use of such materials.

USING COMMERCIALLY PREPARED MATERIALS

Programmed Kits

Programmed kits are produced in a wide range of skill areas, notably reading, math, and study skills. They are designed to help the student gain proficiency by completing problems or examples of certain skills. As he masters each skill, he goes on to a new task until he meets the new challenge. The programmed kit is designed to help the student work independently and to build confidence in his own learning ability. Many are now available for use in intermediate and upper grades. The volunteer is available to encourage the student as he works and to help him as he confronts difficulty. Programmed materials often require record keeping on the part of the student as well as the teacher. A volunteer is most helpful here by facilitating and monitoring records. She is also available to discuss the student's progress with the teacher by reviewing his records.

Worksheets

Worksheets emphasizing specific skills and printed on a master for duplication are useful in programs of individualized instruction. The teacher, after determining the student's needs, provides him with a series of worksheets selected to help him strengthen his skills in an appropriate sequential manner. The student, working independently, completes each worksheet and turns it in for correction. The volunteer, working with the student, may assist with the correction and, at appropriate times, discuss the results with the teacher.

Tapes and Filmstrips

Tapes, filmstrips, and individual-concept films (film loops) are increasing in popularity as aids to instruction. They are frequently used by individual students to help enrich their learning. They become more effective when there are volunteers available to assist the students in their use of the machine, as well as to engage the student in discussion of the content. The students need help in the proper selection of these materials and in locating the filmstrip, tape, or film loop they have chosen. The classroom teacher does not always have the time to assist each student. A volunteer or aide who is familiar with the media materials is helpful to students as they seek help in developing concepts.

Games

Various commercially prepared games designed to reinforce basic skills are available for intermediate and upper grade classroom use. These games frequently require the participation of several persons and need an adult participant to assist the student learners.

Games, when used effectively, can be helpful motivating techniques and are useful in developing logical thinking and meaningful concept development. In addition, they have socializing benefits as they help individuals to interreact with one another.

TEACHER-MADE MATERIALS

Some of the most effective materials in use in intermediate and upper grades, as well as the primary grades, are those developed and prepared by teachers for their students. They are often more relevant and meaningful for the specific group. Volunteers or aides are very helpful in the preparation of these materials because they can relieve the teacher of some of the time-consuming handwork that is required in this task. The help provided may be art work, typing, duplication of materials, and assistance in the collating of instructional materials.

Once the teacher- or pupil-made materials are ready for use by the students, the volunteers and aides can provide the same kind of service they do with commercially prepared instructional aids.

A few of the typical examples of teacher-prepared materials are as follows:

1. Worksheets designed to meet the specific needs of a student or a group of students.
2. Visuals for overhead projection.
3. Mini-lessons prepared to help a student in specific areas and incorporate a variety of media.
4. Charts and graphs.
5. Tapes.
6. Filmstrips and slides.

Volunteers can work with students to develop some of these materials. This is frequently a good motivational technique to use with youngsters who haven't enjoyed much academic success.

AIDING THE SLOWER LEARNER

A student in the intermediate and upper grades who has experienced difficulty in learning the basic skills is often disenchanted with school. He may have given up on himself and frequently can be disruptive to his classmates and teacher. If he is to experience any success at all, he must be provided with materials that are suited to his needs. Other students also termed "slow learners" may not cause discipline problems, but are rather content to come to school and unobtrusively put in their time. Busy teachers often must spend too much time disciplining the disruptive student and are left with too little time to meet the needs of the shy child.

Volunteers can be very helpful in such a situation by working with the students in a variety of ways.

One-to-One Instruction

Isolating a student with an attentive adult will give the slow learner added confidence and help to instill in him a desire to accomplish a task. You must counsel the volunteer to use a positive approach and insure that the student is provided with material that is within his capabilities.

As the volunteer works with the student and progress is noted, discussions with the teacher are necessary to determine a further course of action.

Using Small Groups

Volunteers may work with a small group of youngsters who have similar learning difficulties. A group of three or four students achieving at the same level may gain confidence from the type of interaction provided in small-group instruction.

Using the format of either one-to-one or small-group instruction, a volunteer may work in any of the major subject areas. Specific activities are discussed in further detail in another chapter, but some suggestions for working with older children are listed here.

Reading
1. Language experience activities
2. Reading and listening skill development
3. Vocabulary development
4. Phonetic analysis
5. Extracting main ideas
6. Practice in reading for information
7. Developing word attack skills

Language Arts
1. Practice in identifying parts of speech
2. Practice in sentence writing
3. Discussion of literature
4. Developing spelling skills
5. Choral reading
6. Letter writing

7. Composition writing
8. Developing research skills
9. Outlining skills for note taking

Mathematics

1. Practicing basic math functions
2. Developing skills in math tables
3. Help in learning math terminology
4. Conducting flashcard drills
5. Working with manipulative materials

Science

1. Monitoring experiments
2. Assisting in the laboratory
3. Assisting students doing research
4. Assisting students in developing individual and small-group projects

Social Studies

1. Assisting in research
2. Having discussions based on reading
3. Assisting students in developing individual and small-group projects

SPECIAL-INTEREST CLUBS

Volunteers or aides may be called upon to participate in the operation of special-interest clubs. In some instances the nonprofessionals may lead the clubs if they have sufficient interest or expertise in a certain area.

Clubs may be operated during the school day if there is time available for such an undertaking. A study period or similar block of time may be used for clubs. If the schedule does not allow, special-interest groups could meet after school. Many school systems provide late buses to permit after-school activities of this sort.

The purpose of these clubs is to enable students to pursue an area of high interest for enjoyment as well as enrichment. The number and types of clubs is limited only by the availability of willing and qualified people to lead them.

A staff member should be available as coordinator of

the groups, both for legal reasons and to provide communication between the club leaders and the school administration.

Some typical special interest clubs are discussed here as a possible guide to follow.

Dramatics

Dramatics clubs can involve themselves in every phase of theater presentations. This could include script writing, costume design, scenery and set building, lighting, presentations, publicity discussion groups, and field trips to see legitimate theater performances.

In most communities there are citizens with a theater background who could be recruited to work with these groups. If school funds are not available to support a dramatics group, they could be self-sufficient by putting on performances for the public at a modest ticket price.

Creative Writing

Students who wish to pursue their creative writing skills beyond what is provided in the curriculum may form a club. Poetry, short stories, essays, plays, and novels are all potential topics for consideration. A literary magazine is a possible goal for such a group. The volunteer is available to provide leadership and encouragement to the students as they seek to develop their talents. Students might be encouraged to send their best efforts to newspapers and magazines to be considered for publication.

Arts and Crafts

In some communities artists and craftsmen living in the area donate their time to come into the schools and work with students. The goal of an arts and crafts interest group would be to further develop the skills of the students and to give them added opportunity for creative expression. Activities might include oil and water color painting, sketching, ceramics, pottery, weaving, batik, puppetry, and block printing. Trips to art museums and discussions about artists and their work are also possibilities.

A feature project of the group might be an arts and

crafts show open to the public in which the students are given the opportunity to display their work.

Photography

This is another area where volunteers can be brought in to help enrich the students. Photography clubs can pursue the technical aspects of this profession (i.e., film development and print making), as well as go on picture-taking excursions to test their skills. Discussions on use of equipment, proper picture composition, and lighting are followed up by practical experience.

Film making is becoming an increasingly popular art form among young people. Short films on various topics could be produced by the group.

There is a relationship between each of the groups discussed so far. If each of the groups were to contribute its expertise to a common effort, perhaps a film could result in which the script, scenery, photography, and performance were all club activities.

Coin and Stamp Clubs

Groups meet to discuss, trade, buy, and sell stamps and coins. Most communities have many enthusiastic coin and stamp collectors who could be persuaded to come and work with a group of students.

Astronomy Club

This is a subject which holds great fascination for many people. A key project could be to have the group build its own telescope from component parts. A fairly sophisticated instrument could result with relatively little expense. This group would necessarily have to meet evenings for celestial observation. Special parental permission should be obtained if the group is to meet solely with nonprofessional volunteers.

This is by no means a complete list of potential special interest clubs that could be formed. Suggestions for recruiting volunteers with special skills are discussed more thoroughly in other chapters of this book. It should be noted, however, that it is frequently through participation in groups such as those just described that students make decisions regarding choice of careers.

VOLUNTEERS ASSISTING WITH PROJECTS AND ACTIVITIES

Volunteers and aides can be most helpful to the students in the preparation of projects and similar activities. They may help in gathering materials and provide assistance to the students as they work on projects in the field of science. Similar help in art or social studies projects may also be provided. The volunteer gives guidance and encouragement to the student while acting as liaison with the teacher. This service is particularly valuable when preparing for science fairs and other such major undertakings. The teacher does not always have the time to oversee the efforts of each individual student.

Research-oriented projects that require the student to work away from the classroom are another area for volunteer assistance. A volunteer may work with a group of students as they do research on their chosen topic. The volunteer may also help the student to prepare his presentation by listening to him and suggesting needed changes.

SCHOOL-COMMUNITY COOPERATIVE PROJECTS

School-age youngsters are becoming increasingly more aware of community problems that face the modern world. They frequently become engaged in activities that take them away from the school to do field work. Volunteers can help by providing transportation and accompanying the students as they carry on their projects. Necessary parent permission should be obtained before embarking on such an activity. A sample form for parental permission is included in this chapter.

Some possible community projects are:
1. Clean-up campaign
   a. Clean litter from streets
   b. Clean up public parks
   c. Clean up ponds and streams
   d. Neighborhood cleaning and painting
2. Ecology campaigns
   a. Seek out sources of pollution

    b. Correct sources of erosion
    c. Plant trees and shrubs
    d. Clean up streams and ponds
3. Drug education campaigns
    a. Visit drug rehabilitation facilities
    b. Do volunteer work at centers
    c. Hold discussion groups with interested citizens
    d. Form student-adult groups to help correct drug problems.

VOLUNTEERS ASSISTING IN OTHER AREAS

The use of volunteers and aides in intermediate and secondary grades can be as broad as the needs of the teachers, as well as in enrichment activities. In many instances they may be helpful to the teacher and school administration by assisting in noninstructional areas. Some examples of this type of service are:

1. Teaching classroom housekeeping skills
2. Duplication of materials
3. Preparation of materials
4. Bulletin boards and displays
5. School record keeping
6. Assist in supervisory capacity
    a. cafeteria
    b. playground
    c. bus procedure

SCHOOL-COMMUNITY COOPERATIVE PROJECT

My child _____ has my permission to participate in the School-Community Project. It is my understanding that this project includes field trips and other activities which are conducted away from the school premises. Transportation for these trips will be provided by bus or private car.

Signed _____ [Parent or Guardian] _____

Date

PARENT PERMISSION FORM

Student-to-Student Volunteers

/ **7**

Years ago, when small rural schools functioned with one teacher in a single room, it was common practice for teachers to use the older children to help instruct younger children. Schools are again discovering the value of this procedure. Not only does it provide needed help in individualizing instruction, it has proven to be of great value to the student volunteer. Teaching others is an important way to synthesize one's own learning. The act of imparting knowledge and engendering understanding improves skills in articulation and organization. It also furnishes the volunteer student avenues for broadening his horizons and self-awareness. There are various ways to capitalize on the ready supply of student volunteers. Using secondary students to assist in elementary schools can be a very valuable service if care is taken in the administration of the program.

RECRUITING SECONDARY STUDENT VOLUNTEERS

Most junior and senior high school students are sensitive to the needs of young people for success and happiness in the lower grades. When recruiting student volunteers, you will need to stress the importance of a mature commitment to helping young children obtain success and a wholesome self-image. For this purpose, informational meetings with the candidates are essential.

Before engaging in communication with would-be student volunteers, you must be sure you have genuine support from the high school staff, particularly the administrators. Impress upon them the importance of the program and the value to the secondary student as well as to the young child. When you acquire support, based on an understanding of the benefits of a student volunteer program, it will be easier to surmount the minor problems that occur when arranging transportation, released time, and so on.

It is helpful to have someone on the high school staff serve in a liaison capacity. This person might assist in arranging informational and training sessions, distribute and collect application forms, and maintain lists of participants. Work in conjunction with this person to set up your first meeting with those students who show an interest. The liaison person can announce this meeting through various means, such as the public address system, bulletin boards, or student council.

At this meeting it is helpful to have students or other volunteers to assist you when explaining the many activities in which volunteers engage and the personal experiences that provide gratification. It is important that the motive of the would-be high school volunteer is one of genuine interest on behalf of younger children in need and not just a means of being released from the last period class, or a chance to leave the high school during the day. It is important that the would-be volunteers understand the need to be punctual and regular in their service to the younger children. Young children become attached to the volunteer. They should not have their feelings of trust threatened by inexcusable absences and tardiness. The liaison person and other staff members will be helpful in assuring that those applying are responsible, stable, and sincere.

You may find that high school students who are only average in their studies and sometimes in trouble with the school administration have excellent rapport with young children. They often perform well as volunteers. Academic achievement should not be the only criteria for selection of participants. Possession of a good sense of humor can also indicate potential for success as a volunteer.

[NAME OF SCHOOL]
[City and State]
VOLUNTEER PROGRAM
Student-to-Student
[Big Brother-Big Sister]

The student-to-student program is a program for high school students who wish to work with and befriend an elementary school youngster on a one-to-one basis.

Transportation: You will have to provide your own transportation or ride with a friend in the program. It may be possible for you to ride home on the school bus from the elementary school in which you serve.

Remember, if you sign up for this program, a child will be depending on you *every* day. Don't let him down!

Name_____ Address_____
School_____Home Room_____Telephone
Grade_____

Days Available: Mon._____Tues._____Wed._____
(Please check)   Thurs._____Fri._____

(One day per week is a minimum requirement — more are desirable)

SCHOOL PREFERRED (check below)

Beaver Brook	*Mill Ridge	Roberts-Locust
Great Plain	Morris St.	Shelter Rock
*Hayestown	Park Ave.	South Street
*King Street	*Pembroke	*Stadley Rough

* Please note: Five of the schools are on early dismissal — 2:45 p.m. Dismissal for the remaining schools is 3:15 p.m.

SAMPLE APPLICATION FORM

After you have had an opportunity to identify those secondary students who you feel can contribute to the volunteer program, you will need to concern yourself with such matters as scheduling, possible release time for some students and transportation. In most communities high schools dismiss at an earlier hour than the elementary schools. You may find that this forty-five to sixty minute time period is enough to allow students to get to elementary schools on one or more afternoons each week for at least thirty-minute tutorial periods. It may also be possible for high schools to assign study periods to student volunteers during the last period of the day so that they can leave early enough to allow for at least thirty-minute tutorial periods in the elementary schools. For those who are within easy traveling distance, it may be possible to schedule blocks of time during the day when high school students can be released to work with younger children.

Before assigning high school students to elementary schools, be sure that proper transportation can be arranged. Many high school students drive cars; also elementary schools may be within walking distance. It might also be possible to arrange for a special bus to deliver and pick up volunteers.

Some schools have found that school volunteer work is of such significance that academic credits are given to participants. This practice should be given serious consideration. The natural inclination of many educators might be to consider student participation as valid primarily for those who want to become teachers. It must be realized, however, that the major purpose of a student-to-student volunteer program is to foster in youth a practice of performing needed services to one's community and neighbor, as well as to aid in the operation of school programs.

ONE-TO-ONE TUTORING

High school volunteers can engage in the many tutoring activities as outlined in the previous chapters. These activities can center around such procedures as listening to children read, helping youngsters with homework, and reinforcing math skills. It is important to stress that the high school students' assistance will be more valued when they encourage and explain; they should be discouraged from doing the work for the youngster. It is important for the student volunteer to know that he is a facilitator of learning and his one-to-one contact and counseling may be all that is needed to assist the young child. Most high school students who volunteer for this program give evidence of having much more patience than the adult educators anticipate.

Date

Dear (Student's Name):

I am delighted that you are able to participate in the Student-to-Student (Big Brother-Big Sister) volunteer program. I am assigning you to the elementary school of your choice which is_____School for____[day or days] afternoon(s).

If you will be able to increase this time to include one or more additional afternoons, I hope you will express this to the principal of the above-mentioned school.

The principal of the school has been notified of your desire to participate in this program and is eager to meet you. Kindly report to him on the afternoon designated above.

You will remember that at our meeting on September 21,. I stressed the importance of maintaining the schedule to which you have committed yourself. This is vital for the trust you build with your young friend. When emergencies arise that prohibit you from attendance, be sure to notify the school office.

If you plan to participate in the program during seventh period study, remember that you must bring a note to your housemaster from home giving permission for early dismissal on the days you participate.

We hope this will be a rewarding and creative experience for you.

Most sincerely,

[Volunteer Chairman]

SAMPLE ASSIGNMENT SHEET

BIG BROTHER-BIG SISTER

The act of tutoring young children in academic areas is often secondary to the other benefits derived from involvement of older children working with younger children. The elementary child who needs tutoring is often the child who needs close relationships and understanding. It is not unusual for the young child to look upon his experiences with the high school student as more meaningful than with his teacher. This may be true because of the great differences in age between the young child and the teacher and the changing social patterns. The high school student can and often does find it easier to understand the problems of a young child. It is important to stress this fact to the high school volunteer. He must know that the way he relates to the young child can have a significant impact on that child's development. Stress to the volunteer that when working with young children he must avoid being too critical or negative and that he should praise the young child whenever he can. If the child tends to prefer to talk about himself, the volunteer should be a good listener, even if it means covering less ground in the academics. The rapport he builds with the child will eventually lead to greater achievement in academic growth.

STUDENT VOLUNTEERS AND FOREIGN LANGUAGES IN THE ELEMENTARY SCHOOLS

Educators have often said that one of the best ways to learn is to teach. This is not only true for helping one to better understand concepts, but is also true with skill development through practice. Foreign languages are good examples of this.

There are many who will take a dim view of the practice of using students or adults who are not properly trained to teach young people foreign languages. The authors feel that an elementary foreign language program with student volunteers is possible if done properly.

Unquestionably, the high school students selected for this program will need to be selected with care. In addition to the usual desire to use students who are committed to the concept of helping others and who relate well with others, we suggest the following guidelines:

1. The students considered for participation should have at least three years of the language in secondary schools. This would necessitate the use of older students.
2. The students should be high academic achievers.
3. Their enunciation and pronunciation should be good.
4. They should have a training program before beginning.

Needless to say, the nature of an elementary foreign language program is very sensitive. Care must be taken to avoid the use of students whose pronunciation is faulty. This is especially important because a habit of mispronunciation will be difficult to erase.

One of the difficulties older students and adults have when learning a second language is acquiring the appropriate speech inflection and pronunciation. This problem is less evident when the language student is introduced to the new language at an early age. An elementary school language program is an excellent way to avoid this problem.

You must be sure that those students who are used for instruction are properly trained. It might be advisable to arrange released time for the language teacher or department head. In this time the professional could outline the activities and procedures to be used by the volunteers before the program begins. After the program gets under way, the professional might use this time to supervise the core of student language instructors on a rotating basis.

Another language activity that should be considered is that of junior and senior high school students helping young immigrants who do not speak English. This can be a less formal program than the one outlined above. In this program the student volunteer meets with the newcomer as often as possible and tutors him in English, helps him to understand his school work and homework, and gives him guidance.

When the volunteer knows the student's language, it is particularly helpful in the beginning. He can provide valuable services as an interpreter as well as a tutor. Experience has shown that as the new student begins to become familiar with English, it is not necessarily beneficial to have volunteers who know the learner's language. Indeed, it may sometimes be detrimental because the volunteer and student may rely too heavily on the learner's language. Without a knowledge of the learner's language, the volunteer will require a greater effort of the learner.

Effective English as a Second Language (E.S.L.) programs have been in effect in many communities. Where there are large numbers of children whose first language is one other than English, it is quite possible of a small professional staff to provide the necessary services with the help of student and adult volunteers. In Danbury, Connecticut, two E.S.L. teachers and a group of parent volunteers provide a program that helps more than ninety students in grades one through eight.

CLUB ACTIVITIES

School attendance can often be much more meaningful to children when the school provides programs geared to their special interests and talents. It is often difficult for an overworked staff to provide all of the opportunities that should be provided in these areas. Sometimes there are no members on the school staff with the necessary talents to enrich a program with such activities as:

Creative dramatics	Ecology
Woodworking	Careers
Sewing	Ceramics
Photography	Chess
Astronomy	Music
Puppets	Others

A high school volunteer can provide an excellent service by providing special talents and the time needed to put them to good use. You might want to consider the selection of clubs that can meet during the day or after school hours. Each club could be conducted by one or a team of high school volunteers. These clubs, in addition to those mentioned above might include such areas as:

Coin collecting	Poetry
Stamp collecting	Indian lore
Jazz	Sports (intramurals)
Rock and roll	Others
Science	

The list is endless.

It may be advisable to have the volunteer participate as a one-to-one tutor before his attempting club activities that involve groups of children. You will then be able to determine whether he has established a pattern of dependability and wholesome rapport.

When high school volunteers engage in enrichment and club activities, it may be necessary for you to review the legal aspects surrounding their involvement. This is particularly true when sports activities are involved. Usually, designating a properly certified staff person as an official coordinator is sufficient. However, it may be necessary to insure that this professional is present during the activity and located within easy contact. Sports activities that are inclined to be hazardous, such as tumbling and gymnastics, should not be assigned to high school student volunteers. The legal implications in cases of injuries are far too severe. You might, however, want to use them as assistants to properly certified personnel who supervise these activities.

ONE-TO-ONE VOLUNTEERS WITHIN THE SCHOOL

We have been discussing the value of secondary students working with younger children. Similar programs can be conducted within the same building. Many schools are finding that intermediate grade children are excellent tutors for primary grade children. While the possibilities are fewer, particularly in regard to conducting group activities like clubs, there are many advantages to conducting programs within a building. Where this has been done, it has been found that the time spent on tutoring and other activities was not detrimental to the older child. On the contrary, achievement of the older children tends to increase. Such involvement provides the student volunteer an opportunity to experience success and a feeling of accomplishment which tends to enhance his self-image and motivation.

One way to schedule such activities is to pair a primary teacher with an intermediate grade teacher. Working together they can arrange convenient times when these activities can take place. Some of the most successful of these building activities have been:

1. Listening to children read.
2. Reading to individual and small groups of children.
3. Helping children to write experience stories.
4. Developing hobbies.
5. Helping with simple motor skills like throwing, catching, skipping.
6. Preparing kindergarten children for dismissal.
7. Assisting with audio-visual equipment.

Student volunteers have proven to be a very valuable asset in tutoring and helping younger children; however, the opportunities for assisting in many other facets of school life are endless. We have outlined activities that would be valuable for future teachers. There are many activities that are also practical for future secretaries, mechanics, businessmen, and artists. Students who are exposed to proper office etiquette and procedures through practical experiences in the school office are well along the way to becoming successful secretaries and executives in the business world. Talented art students may be given the responsibility to decorate the school interior with their creative efforts. The results often reflect a cheerful child-oriented atmosphere.

Whatever the activity, an important fact to remember is that a student volunteer program succeeds best when the professionals support the activities and display a positive attitude. Recognition for the students' efforts is most important. The principal or supervisor should make an effort to periodically consult with his young volunteer, advise him in his work, see that his working conditions are pleasant, and most importantly, display a genuine appreciation for his efforts. You might want to consider, for the end of the term, a formal letter of appreciation similar to the following.

Date_____

Dear [Student's Name]:

Another school year is about to end. Through the creative efforts of the children, the staff, and volunteers like you, it has been a productive and successful year.

Please accept my sincere thanks for your help which you gave freely and graciously. It is through this kind of help to others that a community becomes a better place in which to live. You have asked for no material rewards for your efforts as a school volunteer, but the reward that comes through the satisfaction of having been a positive influence on a young person who needed help is a far greater reward. I sincerely hope that you will continue to provide useful community service throughout your adult life.

Hoping you have an enjoyable summer,

Most sincerely,

_____
Principal of School

SAMPLE LETTER OF APPRECIATION

Using Volunteers and Teacher Aides in Reading, Language Arts, and Mathematics

8

The subject matter involved in the teaching of reading, language arts, and mathematics is not only the basis of much of the school curriculum, but it also lends itself to the use of volunteer and paraprofessional assistance. Since the classroom teacher must spend a good part of her time helping students improve skills in these areas, help in carrying out these activities would be most useful.

In this chapter some specific activities and exercises that volunteers and aides may use in working with students are discussed. The emphasis will be on the kinds of learning skills that volunteers and aides may help the students to master. Most of these skills can best be acquired through the effective use of individual or small-group instructional techniques. Whether the teacher chooses to utilize her assistants to work with students or to help in the preparation of materials is a matter of her choice. Either way the students are sure to benefit.

READING ACTIVITIES FOR VOLUNTEERS AND AIDES

It is a widely accepted fact that an essential to learning is a positive self-image on the part of the learner. He must believe that he can be successful and this belief must be reinforced by those working with him.

One of the primary values of the volunteer-aide concept is that it permits a greater opportunity for interaction between the student and the tutor. It is with this in mind that you should always prepare the volunteer for her tasks by encouraging her to use a positive approach. As stated in the previous chapter, the volunteer-aide should always praise the student for his efforts and urge him to continue to try to do well. This approach to learning is very important in the development of reading skills. The task of learning to read is one of the most difficult challenges a student faces in his formal education.

If a child looses his confidence as a reader, it becomes an overwhelming deterrent to learning progress in other areas. A volunteer or aide should, when working with young learners, keep the following factors in mind:

1. A healthy, positive self-concept is a prerequisite to learning.
2. The act of listening to a child implies that you accept him as a worthwhile person.
3. The child will develop a better sense of self-worth if you praise him for his efforts rather than deride him for his failures.
4. Provide him with tasks at which he can succeed. As he masters these, move on to the next level.
5. Take the time to know the student as a person. Your interest in him bolsters his confidence in your relationship.

The specific activities in which a volunteer or aide may be helpful vary with the age and level of the individual student. Activities are described on the basis of reading developmental skills rather than by grade or age levels. Some examples of these skill levels are:

1. Readiness
2. Decoding skills
3. Comprehension

4. Reading for information
5. Reading for pleasure

READINESS SKILL ACTIVITIES

Reading readiness is not determined by chronological age or I.Q. It is rather the acquisition of the skills and feelings necessary to be ready to learn to read using one of the conventional programs.

The volunteer or aide can assist the teacher in preparing the students for reading by helping them in some of the following readiness activities:

1. Following directions
2. Letter recognition
3. Language and speech development
4. Physical capability
   a. visual discrimination
   b. auditory discrimination
5. Experiences
6. Social skills
7. Learning about books
8. Being read to

Following Directions

Knowing how to follow directions expedites the learning-to-read process by helping the youngster to function in the formal reading program. A volunteer working with individuals or small groups of students may give them help in developing their skills by giving such simple directions as: "Paul, please bring me the yellow pencil from your desk," or "All the girls wearing red may come to the front."

As the level of skill is determined and mastered, the directions may become more involved, eventually involving a series of steps. Most youngsters have learned how to follow simple directions by the time they enter school, however, additional practice is often needed to help the children reach the goal of understanding and retaining directions over a long period of time.

Letter Recognition

A youngster preparing to read must be familiar with the alphabet and be able to distinguish letters from other symbolic forms. Volunteers may work with students using alphabet charts and letter flashcards to help the children to gain these skills. Exercises based on identifying and isolating letters from printed word cards can be conducted by volunteers. Worksheets are another technique that may be used. Students can be asked to identify letters from bulletin board signs or from everyday objects such as the children's milk cartons found around the classroom. Sandpaper letters and a sand tray for drawing letters with the fingers are also helpful aids.

Language and Speech Development

Children must be encouraged to express ideas as part of the reading process. Volunteers can be used to carry on discussions with small groups. The emphasis should be on helping youngsters to develop vocabulary and to confidently relate their ideas to others. This activity is particularly important to children to whom English is a second language. Topics for discussion should be such familiar subjects as family, pets, hobbies, or play activities. The role of the discussion leader is to encourage each student to participate and to be sure that all students practice good listening skills.

Physical Capabilities

Visual and auditory discrimination skills are integral to the reading process. Volunteers can be most helpful here by assisting the teacher in assessing the skills of individual students. This can be done by observing the student as he works with some of the activities described in this chapter. The teacher may also instruct the volunteer in the use of some of the skill inventories available for determining visual and auditory discrimination skills.

The volunteer may also be alerted to other signs of physical development such as motor skills, stamina, and general health.

Experiences

Many youngsters come to school with a deficit of life experiences. Some of these can be compensated for by having volunteers provide the youngsters with the opportunities to engage in painting, simple dramatics, wood working, and other related activities.

Pictures, books, film strips, and discussions can also be used to help fill the gaps in the child's developmental background. There is, of course, no substitute for home-originated life experiences. However, exposure to a variety of activities and opportunities of this nature will give the youngster greater confidence as he prepares to become a reader.

Social Skills

Each of the activities previously mentioned will help the youngster to develop the social skills necessary to participate in a reading program. He must learn such things as how to relate to other children, to take part in group activities, to function as a part of a group, to perform the basic routines of the class, and to function in a structured situation within a system of rules.

Learning About Books

A beginning reader should be familiar with the "anatomy" of a book. The volunteer can conduct activities designed to help the students learn about books. He should know such things as the terminology used to describe a book, i.e., page, cover, front, and back can be discussed. Left to right progression should be introduced. Students should be given the chance to handle books and to look through them. Questions about books should be encouraged.

Reading to Students

As mentioned in an earlier chapter, a most important function that may be provided by volunteers or aides is that of reading to the students. This not only provides the student with the desire to learn to read, but it also helps to give him some of the experiences he will use in developing his reading skills.

DECODING SKILLS

The term "decoding" refers to the child's ability to recognize words and the printed symbols that represent their sounds. The essence of decoding is, of course, letters and the sounds they indicate. The elements to be considered are:

1. Letters of the alphabet
2. Sounds of the alphabet
   a. consonants
   b. vowels
3. Letter blends
4. Syllables
5. Prefixes
6. Suffixes
7. Sight vocabulary

These skills are taught beginning in the primary grades and continuing throughout formal reading instruction. Volunteers and aides can be part of this process working with students under the guidance of the teacher.

Alphabet

Many materials such as flash cards, charts, oral games, kinesthetic cards, and blocks are available to assist in the instruction of the alphabet. As the child learns the letters, he may work with volunteers to reinforce his skills and to learn the various symbols for upper and lower case. Worksheet exercises are useful in helping the youngsters to utilize their skills and to build confidence.

Sounds of the Alphabet

Teacher-made tapes are a useful technique for teaching phonetic skills. Volunteers or aides can assist in the preparation of these tapes and monitor their use by the students. If recording equipment is not available, oral exercises based on vowel and consonant sounds are useful. The student should be encouraged to verbalize the sounds and to practice them often.

Letter Blends

Picture cards, worksheets, and word lists are a few of the materials that volunteers or aides may use. Many games and activities may be used as a basis for a small-group lesson.

Syllables, Prefixes, and Suffixes

Word lists, charts, crossword puzzles, whole sentences, worksheets, tapes, filmstrips, pictures, and workbooks can all be used effectively by volunteers and aides to help youngsters acquire these skills.

Sight Vocabulary

Some words may not be learned easily using the other decoding techniques. These words must be learned as a whole word and they must be recognized by the reader when he sees them.

Many prepared word lists are commercially available for use by schools. In addition to these, teachers may develop their own lists based on the needs of the students. Volunteers working in small groups or with single students can provide extra help to those students who are developing these skills.

COMPREHENSION

Reading without understanding has very little value. Teachers spend much of their reading instruction time working to help their students increase their reading comprehension. Such importance is attached to this skill that large sections of standard reading and achievement tests are based on comprehension.

Many reading exercises designed to improve comprehension can easily be monitored by a volunteer or aide. Diagnostic screening based on reliable instruments is a necessary prerequisite to determining a plan of action to be followed by the teacher and her assistants. Some activities that are frequently used in the area of comprehension are:

1. Questions based on short paragraphs.
2. Oral summaries of short excerpts.
3. Discussions based on the reading of passages.
4. Interpretation of literature.
5. Following written directions for specific activities.

READING FOR INFORMATION

A typical application of reading skills is to read for specific information or facts. This is a skill that requires the student to isolate and retain key elements as he peruses the written material. It is the essence of most reading that is carried on in academic pursuits. Many exercises are helpful to students as they strive to improve this skill. Some of these are as follows:

1. Locating specific information in an encyclopedia.
2. Selecting key sentences from passages.
3. Using special materials such as dictionaries, maps, subject-oriented textbooks.
4. Seeking answers to questions prepared from written material.

READING FOR PLEASURE

The ultimate result of all reading instruction is a student who enjoys reading for the pleasure it gives him. If this goal is to be achieved, the young student must be exposed to a variety of literature. Time must be set aside each day for the children to select some reading material and quietly enjoy it.

As the child is developing skills, he will benefit from being read to. Volunteers and aides can perform this service, as well as help youngsters select their own reading material. Often aides or volunteers may be available to help the children with their reading and to discuss what they have read. An important service that they provide in this area is to expedite the selection of reading matter for the youngsters.

VOLUNTEERS AND AIDES IN MATHEMATICS

Modern mathematics programs are designed to use many manipulative materials as well as a variety of printed matter. Teachers frequently plan their lessons for small-group or individual instruction. Math skill levels within a classroom may vary greatly. Diagnostic testing, as well as teacher judgment, are necessary prerequisites to the establishment of a volunteer-aide, student-help program. When you have determined the needs of your students, you can establish your program and decide where the volunteers and paraprofessionals can be of most help to your students.

The activities to be conducted vary with the age and skill level of the students. Younger children usually require more manipulative materials, whereas older students frequently need assistance in learning mathematical tables and practice in various number functions.

Manipulative Materials

Most manipulative materials can be acquired quite inexpensively by substituting common items for those produced commercially. Volunteers and aides can assume this responsibility. Some items that may be used in math programs are: coins, buttons, ice-cream sticks, beans, pebbles, bottle caps, blocks, pipe cleaners, straws, tongue depressors, pencils, cards, marbles, pegs, and similar items that are small and easy for little fingers to handle. Enough of these materials should be gathered for use by at least one group at a time.

Recent textbooks generally suggest a multitude of activities that are helpful to students as they grasp new concepts. Volunteers and aides could help students as they learn the basic number functions and concepts. The materials listed above are useful in teaching sets and groups, as well as the basic mathematical processes.

Tutorial Help for Older Students

In upper grades many students progress more slowly in math because they don't know the mathematical tables. A volunteer could help these students by conducting drill techniques that are done frequently by the teacher. Flashcard games, multiplication tables worksheets, and oral repeat exercises are a few of the activities that could be conducted. By working with students who have difficulty mastering mathematical concepts on a one-to-one basis, volunteers often achieve remarkable success.

Volunteers and Aides Assisting Teachers

Math instruction produces a large volume of paper work that must be dealt with. The student's work needs to be corrected, assessed, and the results shared with the students and then used in planning future activities. A volunteer or an aide can be helpful in the correction of papers. It is, of course, the responsibility of the teacher to make professional judgments of the student's work, including the discussion of his progress. However, a volunteer certainly may be utilized to free the teacher for those tasks by performing the more mechanical functions.

Nonteaching jobs related to math, such as worksheet preparation, worksheet duplication, the setting up of a materials table, and the operation of audio-visual equipment are easily assumed by aides or volunteers after they have been given proper training.

USING VOLUNTEERS AND AIDES IN LANGUAGE ARTS

Language arts instruction can be exciting or it can be a dull and monotonous experience for the student. This learning atmosphere is determined by the approach taken by the teacher. Language arts is ideal for activity-centered instruction using small groups. There are many facets of this subject area that can be utilized by the creative teacher to enliven instruction.

Language arts encompasses both spoken and written expression, creative literature and drama, as well as grammar and syntax. A teacher faced with the task of preparing for this type of instruction must consider all options available and choose those that will be meaningful as well as enjoyable to the students.

One option available to the teacher is to choose to use volunteers or aides to help in the instruction of language arts. The use of supportive nonprofessionals enables the teacher to work more easily with various groups engaging in a wider assortment of activities.

There are many ways in which a volunteer or an aide may be helpful. Some of these activities are:

1. Tutoring on a one-to-one basis.
2. Creative writing with small groups.
3. Assisting in creative dramatics.
4. Worksheet preparation and correction.
5. Practice in essay writing.
6. Helping students prepare and practice speeches.
7. Assisting in the language arts center.
8. Helping students improve handwriting skills.

Tutoring on a One-to-One Basis

The volunteer or aide may help the individual student in a variety of ways. The following are a few examples:

1. Assistance with homework.
2. Practice with parts of speech.
3. Discussion with students based on reading of literature.
4. Discussion of student's written work.

Creative Writing with Small Groups

The volunteers or aides could work with a small group of students in developing creative writing projects. The students could work on such activities as short stories, plays, poetry, or scripts for puppet shows or skits. The major role of the assistant is to provide the students with encouragement and to help them with the coordination of their joint efforts. If the results of their work are to be shared with the total group, the volunteer-aide could help the group to prepare their presentation.

Assisting in Creative Dramatics

Much has been said on this topic in other chapters. It is mentioned here because creative dramatics is part of the language arts curriculum. The volunteer or aide may help in all phases of creative dramatics. This includes everything from script preparation to the actual direction of the presentation. The skills and interests of the nonprofessional assistant are the determining factors in regard to how much they may participate.

Worksheet Preparation and Correction

Volunteers or aides help teachers by preparing worksheets for use in language arts instruction. The teacher provides the content and the materials and the volunteer does the typing and the duplication of the material. When the students have completed the worksheets, the nonprofessional may aid in the correction. The corrected papers are then returned to the teacher who discusses the results with the students.

Practice in Essay Writing

As the student develops his reading and writing skills, he may be given the task of preparing an essay. A volunteer or aide could assist the student in such things as topic selection, research, development of theme, and refinement of final copy. Frequently, the paraprofessional teacher may be helpful by discussing the development of the theme with the student. As he reflects upon his efforts, the student may find ways to polish and refine his work.

Helping Students Prepare and Present Speeches

The assistance given here is similar to that in essay writing. In addition to those suggestions discussed previously, the volunteer or aide helps the student by listening to the student practice his speech in order to get the proper timing, inflection, and to polish the text. He may also assist the student in doing the research for writing the speech.

Assisting in the Language Arts Center

Many schools have a language arts center with a full-time specialist. An aide or volunteer assigned to that area could assist the specialist in diagnostic testing and by working with individual students in skill development. The service provided by a language arts facility could be greatly expanded by the full-time assignment of either a teacher's aide or volunteer.

Assisting Students in Developing Handwriting Skills

Volunteer aides may take the responsibility for handwriting instruction. Through the use of a handwriting book, the nonprofessional could work with those students having the greatest need for further handwriting practice. This would free the teacher to work with the remainder of the class on other activities.

Volunteers and/or aides employed in the instruction of language arts, reading, and mathematics have much to offer for program improvement. As in all areas of instruction, the busy teacher will find much use for nonprofessionals in meeting the needs of her students.

CONCLUSION

We have discussed the use of volunteers and aides in reading, language arts, and mathematics in this chapter. The possibilities for expanding on the suggestions here are endless. Indeed, volumes might be devoted to the subject. Our concentration on subjects that rely heavily on skill development has been deliberate. Many of the suggestions, however, might also be applied to other subjects such as social studies or science.

Volunteers and Aides Assisting in School Management

/ **9**

There are many noninstructional tasks in the operation of a school program that require the efforts of teachers and administrators. These tasks include clerical as well as supervisory assignments necessary for the smooth functioning of a school. They also, however, often create excessive demands on the time and energy of the professional staff.

Most of these noninstructional tasks can be ably performed by volunteers or paraprofessionals if they are properly trained. These assignments include such activities as lunchroom and playground supervision, typing and clerical assistance, food preparation, school crossing supervision, health program assistance, audio-visual materials preparation, handbook preparation, and many more. Each school has its own unique needs and undoubtedly you could add to this list other volunteer assignments at your school.

This chapter includes some suggestions for the effective use of volunteers and aides in noninstructional assignments. It also includes some cautions regarding state and local legal regulations pertaining to the use of nonprofessionals in supervisory positions.

SOME CAUTIONS TO CONSIDER

When you use nonprofessional personnel in a supervisory capacity, you must be aware of the state and local regulations pertaining to school responsibility. In some states it may be legal to assign volunteers and aides the responsibility for the supervision of a lunchroom or playground. In other localities it may be possible to use aides or volunteers only in a capacity of assistance to certified personnel.

Contracts with teacher organizations and local regulations of boards of education are also matters that must be considered. They may restrict the use of nonprofessionals or, on the other hand, they may indicate that teachers are to be freed of all noninstructional responsibilities. Such factors will influence your planning when you consider the use of volunteers or aides in supervisory positions. You must also consider such things as group size, facilities, student attitudes, and safety.

Aides and volunteers, when properly used in supervisory positions, can extend the effectiveness of the professional staff. There are many ways in which you may improve your overall program if aides or volunteers are given the responsibility for the noninstructional tasks that are essential, yet do not require professional skills.

A VOLUNTEER-AIDE HEALTH PROGRAM

Many schools do not have nurses assigned to their staff on a full-time basis. Often the school nurse is required to serve several schools. The nurse has many clerical duties in addition to administering to the health needs of her students.

Volunteers may be called in to help her in the performance of her duties. If you are fortunate enough to have trained nurses as volunteers, they may be assigned to your health facility on a regularly scheduled basis. You may also discover that some of the volunteers are trained in first aid. People with this training certainly are capable of repairing the many scrapes, bruises, and bumps that occur regularly in all schools.

A list of suggestions for using volunteers or aides in the health program might include such things as:

1. Assist the school nurse in weighing and measuring students.
2. Assist the school nurse in the examination of eyesight and hearing.
3. Assist the school nurse in immunization and vaccination programs (polio, rubella, time test, etc.).
4. Assist the school nurse in the clerical duties involved in a health program (typing, filing, health records, etc.).
5. Perform simple first aid when there is no nurse available.
6. Volunteer professionals (doctors, nurses, dentists, etc.) meet with students and discuss good health practices.
7. Volunteer nurse to assume nursing responsibilities in lieu of regular school nurse.
8. Volunteer professionals establish a part-time health or dental clinic for needy students.
9. Assist the school in its efforts on behalf of good nutrition.
10. Provide appropriate health and hygiene counseling where necessary.

PROVIDING FOOD SERVICE WITH VOLUNTEERS

If your school does not have a regular school lunch program with paid employees, you might consider establishing one with volunteers. With proper planning and acquisition of equipment, perhaps through fund raising, a good hot lunch program can be put into operation. Volunteers are used to prepare and serve meals to the students. Most school lunch programs are eligible for a governmental subsidy. Youngsters are charged a nominal fee for each meal to help defray the cost of the food service.

Volunteers may be arranged for on a regularly scheduled basis. You may choose to use a different team of cooks and helpers each day. It is best, however, to use food service volunteers to supplement a paid staff of at least one person to insure a consistent food program and smooth operation. Some of the tasks food service volunteers may perform are:

1. Assist in the preparation of food.
2. Assist in serving the food to youngsters.
3. Assume the responsibility for cleaning tables between lunch periods and after the last period.
4. Assist in the clean-up in the kitchen.
5. Sell tickets or collect money for lunches and milk.
6. Collect tickets or money from the students as they enter the lunchroom.
7. Prepare menus and distribute them to the students.
8. Assist the young children with their utensils and food.
9. Make the dining experience for children homelike and pleasant.

ASSISTING IN SCHOOL OFFICE ROUTINES

Volunteers or aides can be most helpful in assisting the school office staff. This is especially true during periods of peak activity, such as budget or scheduling time. Volunteers can be recruited to type, file, answer phones, and perform other routine activities.

By using volunteers or aides to do some of the routine tasks, the secretary can be freed to assist in preparing budgets, take inventory, or order materials. Such tasks require specialized skills and are very time consuming.

Some office activities in which volunteers or aides may be employed are:

1. Typing materials for teachers and other professional staff members.
2. Operating copying and duplicating machines and other office equipment.
3. Filing materials and information.
4. Filling in for the secretary during her lunch hour.
5. Preparing correspondence to be sent home.

6. Checking in material and supply orders.
7. Maintaining school and student records.
8. Preparing student transfer records for mailing.
9. Marking or stamping new books and other materials.
10. Preparing attendance and lunch statistics.
11. Distributing supplies and materials.
12. Providing school tours for new students and parents.
13. Stocking and supplying the office with materials.

USING VOLUNTEERS FOR EFFECTIVE PUBLIC RELATIONS

Volunteers can be most helpful in improving the public image of a school. They can be used effectively to help the communication process. They can organize informal social gatherings to help publicize a program that you may be in the process of establishing. Parent volunteers might also contribute their typing skills and writing talents to the production of a school newspaper or other periodical.

Parent volunteers can be most helpful in forming telephone calling teams to encourage citizens to vote on important school referendums. This same technique could be used to publicize school and P.T.A. sponsored functions.

Parent volunteers and aides who are having successful and fulfilling experiences working with youngsters in the classroom will be providing excellent public relations just through word-of-mouth contacts in the community. This is one of the many positive fringe benefits that are part of the volunteer program.

AIDING IN PLAYGROUND SUPERVISION

When using volunteers or aides for a supervisory role on the playground, you must be sure there are clearly established rules and regulations. The students, as well as the volunteers and paraprofessionals, must be aware of these rules. They should also be aware of the part they play in the observance and enforcement of them.

The nonprofessional supervisor must be given a specific assignment in performing playground duty. The amount of responsibility allocated depends upon the circumstances. If the volunteer or aide is used in support of a professional, then he is primarily another pair of eyes and hands to monitor and organize activities and report problems to the teacher on duty. A nonprofessional in these circumstances should be encouraged to use reasonable judgment in settling disputes between children or in reacting to potentially dangerous situations. The teacher, of course, has the final responsibility and is usually the one who is called upon for disciplinary action. The advantage of using volunteers or aides under these circumstances is that the playground can safely be supervised using a minimum of teachers. Frequently, there is difficulty in scheduling teacher duty periods within the guidelines of teacher contracts and state laws, which often mandate duty-free periods in the work day for teachers.

When circumstances permit you to use volunteers or aides in lieu of teachers, the proper training of these people is essential. They must learn that good playground supervision requires alertness at all times to possible hazards and situations that require improved safety measures. It is important that the playground aide or volunteer move about so that all activities can be monitored with sufficient frequency to reduce the possibilities for outbreaks of antisocial behavior and unsafe practices. Without proper orientation, poor supervision may result, causing more harm than good. A practice you should guard against is one where playground supervisors gather together to chat while supervising. This often results in diverting attention away from proper supervision. In instances like this, two or three supervisors can be less effective than one person whose attention is not diverted.

The nonprofessional supervisor must also have a good line of communication with the school administration. The volunteers need the support and the supervision of the school principal and staff as they perform their duties. Without your aid and support, the children being supervised may not perceive the supervision in an appropriate light.

AIDING IN LUNCHROOM SUPERVISION

Supervisory assistance by aides or volunteers in the lunchroom requires the same preparation and training as do playground programs. Usually the nonprofessional is assigned to help a teacher in the effective supervision of the lunchroom. The assistant must be familiar with the general rules of conduct, as well as the serving and clean-up procedures. The volunteer or aide helps the students in the serving line and then monitors the groups as they eat. Any problems or significant rule infractions that occur are usually brought to the attention of the teacher on duty. The aide or volunteer can assist with minor problems, but discipline is usually the responsibility of the professional. Many schools, however, have been very successful with lunch programs supervised solely by paraprofessionals. Success in situations like these depends on careful staff selection and training.

It is important to emphasize to volunteers in charge of lunchrooms or playgrounds that their regular attendance is essential. If they are unable to come to school for the day, they must call well ahead of time so that other arrangements can be made.

CLERICAL ASSISTANCE TO TEACHERS

Volunteers or aides can be employed to relieve the teachers of many of their clerical and record-keeping tasks. The teacher is responsible for the compilation and evaluation of data pertaining to students. The nonprofessional can be helpful in recording and filing their data. Some clerical tasks that volunteers can assume are:

1. Recording biographical data on cumulative record file cards.
2. Recording standard test scores on file cards.
3. Recording grades in record book.
4. Operating duplicating and copying machines.
5. Assisting with class attendance.
6. Collecting milk and lunch money.

7. Providing the teacher with typing service.
8. Maintaining the supplies needed in the classroom.
9. Filing and arranging materials, worksheets, etc.
10. Correcting tests or other assignments.

ESTABLISHING SAFETY PROGRAMS

Volunteers can serve as crossing guards to help students cross busy streets. In many cases, a policeman may be provided for the immediate vicinity of the school, but not for other streets further away. You can encourage parents to organize a crossing guard team for each of their streets. They may be invited into the school to participate in a safety program. You might seek the assistance of the police department in this endeavor because proper training is very important. Another important factor to stress is the need to develop in crossing guard volunteers the ability to be pleasant while being firm.

PREPARATION OF SCHOOL HANDBOOK

Volunteers can be used to compile and prepare for publication a school handbook for the parents. This contains useful information designed to answer questions about school routines, philosophy, academic requirements, health requirements, and other information.

In preparing this handbook, the volunteers work under the direction of the school administration. They can do all the typing and layout work necessary before sending it to the printer. If it is to be published by the school, the volunteers can prepare the stencils, run off the copies, collate, and staple the material into booklet form. They can also be given the responsibility for publicizing and distributing the finished product.

CONCLUSION

When aides and volunteers are used in the various areas of school management covered in this chapter, they provide services that can help the school to be more efficient and responsive to the needs of students and families. We have outlined only some of the ways in which they can serve. There are many more. One must realize that the use of aides and volunteers in these areas requires the same kind of effort in training and orientation as is made on behalf of those who work in the classrooms and in academic programs. Experiences related to the kinds of duties the aide or volunteer performs in school that they have acquired in the business or professional world are, indeed, valuable. They provide expertise that can be a creative influence on the operation of a school. Schools, however, need to have particular procedures and an environment that takes into account the physical, social, emotional, and intellectual growth of children. Attitudes and various codes of behavior that might be acceptable in other walks of life may not be suitable for the school milieu. Extra care must be taken to insure that those who assist in the office and elsewhere in the school use the utmost discretion in their dealings with students, parents, and others. The good done by a conscientious staff can be undone when an aide or volunteer exercises poor judgment while dealing with children or parents. This can also happen when they discuss certain activities and personal information indiscreetly with those who either should not be privy to such information or who should receive it from an appropriate professional. With proper care this will not be a problem, and the improved public relations will be a great asset for your efforts.

Enriching the Creative Arts with Volunteers / **10**

Most people would agree that the best schools provide their students with opportunities for more than the acquisition of factual knowledge. All schools include in their philosophy of education the goal to prepare young people to become useful citizens in the community and to live a life of self-worth and gratifying fulfillment. It is well known that today's wage earners are working fewer and fewer hours at their jobs and having longer vacations. It is predicted that even more leisure time will soon be a reality. Educators and boards of education know that more needs to be done to help young people prepare for a meaningful adulthood — an adulthood that will allow time for creative pursuits and interests that do not, of necessity, relate to their careers.

One of the major reasons for the delay in providing appropriate programs to enrich the academic and vocational efforts is the lack of funds. Budget items for broadening cultural and creative arts activities beyond the usual art and music classes are often among the first to be eliminated when budget cuts are imposed. We are not yet at a point where expenditures for such programs can favorably compete with school maintenance, transportation costs, salaries, school supplies, and other traditional expenses. Volunteers can be a valuable source of enrichment in the lives of young people and improve their prospects for a more rewarding adult life.

THEATER EXPERIENCES FOR STUDENTS WITH VOLUNTEER AID

In most communities, there is a large percentage of families who rarely, if ever, attend live theater performances. Where this is true, the children in such families usually do not become playgoers when they become adults, nor do their children who follow them. An introduction to professional theater and other cultural activities during the school years can make a profound difference to these children and bring about wholesome changes in them.

There are many ways to bring good theater to students. Performances can be brought to each school, or children can be transported to performances. In Danbury, Connecticut, parent volunteers who have formed the "On Stage Inc." program, arrange transportation for all elementary and junior high school students to the 1,200-seat high school auditorium. They have found it to be less expensive to pay for buses than to bring individual performances to each school. The experience of children traveling to the professional performance and sitting in a large auditorium, they have found, is a more meaningful theater activity. It becomes a memorable experience, not just a good school assembly program. You will want to decide on the kinds of arrangements that best fit your needs based on costs, suitability of performances, and other factors.

If you feel that it is desirable to have children go to the theater production rather than arrange for the production to come to the school, it is important that the volunteers make suitable transportation arrangements, careful plans for seating, and appropriate procedures for moving large numbers of children in and out of a large auditorium or theater with a minimum of confusion. The following set of instructions might help you to outline the procedures necessary to insure a smooth operation.

Fund Raising for Theater Productions

While it might be possible to rely on volunteer professional creative arts performances, full productions are rarely free. There are many ways in which funds can be raised. Perhaps the simplest is to send a written appeal with an empty return envelope to each home. The appeal might be for an amount slightly higher than the actual per pupil cost to offset those who do not choose to contribute. (Sample letters follow.)

Another fund-raising approach is to solicit annual contributions from local businesses and individuals who are willing to support efforts that foster an appreciation of the theater. The usual school bazaars, fairs, and sales are other possible sources of funds. Your school or school district might wish to engage in more than one approach for obtaining the necessary funds.

Because of the financial nature of this kind of volunteer program, it is wise to do whatever is necessary to protect the people who participate. To cite an example, it might be wise to have an attorney (perhaps, a volunteer) draw up incorporation papers. If large sums of money are handled, bonding might be in order.

Individual Volunteer Performances

There are active professional performers and artists living in virtually every part of the country. Performing live before a young audience is often a very gratifying experience for many artists. Many will perform as a public service whether or not they have children in the school.

A principal recently read in his local newspaper that a resident of the town was preparing for a piano concert at Town Hall in New York. After mustering the necessary courage, he telephoned her to offer her an opportunity to "rehearse" before a school audience. To his surprise, she was delighted to take his offer and has performed for several school audiences since.

There may be musical or theatrical groups in your area that would be pleased to perform for the school without pay. Sometimes an inquiry of a local musicians' or actors' union can prove beneficial. Some of these unions set aside funds to enable performers to conduct free programs for civic, non-profit organizations. This practice furnishes employment for their members, provides a useful community service, and helps to promote future utilization of their services provided by their craft.

DANBURY PUBLIC SCHOOLS
Danbury, Connecticut

Date _____

Dear Parents:

This year's ON STAGE presentation for grades 1 through 6 will be The National Theatre Company's production of Tom Sawyer, a musical version of the famous adventure story to be seen April 3, May 18 and 30. As part of the shool curriculum, your child will go to the performance at the Danbury High School Auditorium by bus during school hours with his teacher.

The sponsor, ON STAGE, is a service of the Danbury Public School Volunteer Program. ON STAGE is supported by voluntary contributions from parents for pupil transportation and the performing group.

All children will attend. The cost is approximately $1.00 per student. Please send your donation to school with your child in the accompanying envelope, or mail it to the Administration Building.

The Danbury Public School System welcomes the help of the volunteers to enrich the lives of all our children through cultural experiences.

Sincerely yours,

_____
Superintendent of Schools

_____
Chairman, School Volunteers

SAMPLE LETTER TO PARENTS

DANBURY PUBLIC SCHOOLS VOLUNTEER PROGRAM
Danbury, Connecticut

Date_____

TO: Elementary School Principals
FROM: Appropriate School Administrator or Volunteer
           Leader
SUBJECT: *ON STAGE*

ON STAGE volunteers will visit classrooms on Monday, March 13, to distribute the accompanying letter to the children in grades 1-6. Be sure to let your teachers know they are coming. Boxes of letters will be delivered to each school by courier on March 9 or 10.

The letters will start the fund-raising campaign for this year's performances (see enclosed letter). The campaign will be concentrated over three weeks ending March 30. Please be sure to send money collected to the Administration Office by courier *daily*.

If your School Newsletter is going out to parents before March 13, you might want to mention that the children will be bringing home the *ON STAGE* letter.

You will be advised of your performance schedules and bus pickups at a later date.

Enc.

SAMPLE INSTRUCTIONS TO THE PRINCIPALS

Conducting School Productions with Volunteers

Are there retired or former theater people in or around your community? A check might result in several possible volunteers. Some schools have successfully used such people to direct activities as well as perform in schools. Attending good theater performances as indicated above can help to foster a life-long appreciation of dramatics. Firsthand experience through performing, however, can be more effective. We develop a keener appreciation for plays in which

[NAME OF SCHOOL DISTRICT]
[Town, State]

Date _____

TO: Elementary Principals
FROM: Theater Production Volunteer Chairman
SUBJECT: Directions for the Theater Production on
           May 18.

BUS SCHEDULE	NAME OF SCHOOL	NUMBER OF BUSES
Thurs. May 18	Mill Ridge	14 buses First 14 buses in line
10:00 a.m. pickup		
at school	Morris St.	6 buses Last 6 buses in line
10:30 a.m. performance		

PICKUP LOCATION
AFTER PERFORMANCES

All Morris Street students will
exit in the back of the auditorium
to load the last six buses in line.

Mill Ridge School — Orchestra
section closest to the stage will
leave by the stage exit and load
the first buses in line. The Mill
Ridge balcony section and rear
of auditorium will exit by the
back of the auditorium.

Thurs. May 18	Roberts Ave. School	7 buses First 7 buses in line
12:30 p.m. pickup		
at school		
1:00 p.m. performance	Park Ave.	9 buses Last 9 buses in line

All Roberts Ave. students will
leave by the stage exit to load
the first 7 buses.

All Park Avenue students will
leave by the back of the auditorium and load the last nine buses
in line.

Please Note:
1. The buses in which you arrive for the performance may not be the same buses in which you will leave.
2. Each school has been assigned a sufficient number of buses to carry the children to the auditorium.
3. We should keep in mind that during this period of day there are classes in session at the high school.
4. Be ready to begin loading the buses at your pickup time 10:00 a.m. or 12:30 p.m.

Seating in the Auditorium

May 18 — 10:30 a.m. performance

Mill Ridge School — All seats in balcony; Rows F through Z in center section of auditorium and rows A through Z in left section of auditorium (facing stage).

Morris Street School — All seats on the right of auditorium (facing stage) and rows A through E in center section of the auditorium.

May 18 — 1:00 p.m. performance

Roberts Ave. School — Left section of auditorium (facing stage) and rows A through K in center section.

Park Ave. School — Rows L through Z in center section of auditorium; all seats on the right (facing stage) and the balcony.

General Information

1. It is recommended that each principal be with his school group attending the performances.
2. There will be no need for the teacher to invite parents to assist. The quality of the production should take care of most potential disciplinary problems.
3. There will be no room for special guests.
4. Items like candy and chewing gum *will not be allowed. PLEASE BE SURE.*
5. If you have a handicapped child needing special care, please let me know so that special arrangements can be made.

we were involved in the past. The interpretation of roles and the play's message become more meaningful. Great works are easier to understand and enjoy when we can draw upon a background of involvement, even if the involvement was on a less sophisticated level.

We have already discussed the use of volunteers in after-school dramatics clubs. You might also consider their use for regular school hours by using their services in dramatics to augment the regular language arts and English curricula. This approach often makes school a more gratifying experience for many students who might otherwise have negative attitudes.

There are theater experiences that appropriate volunteers can provide that may not be possible without them. Many schools cannot afford to provide the proper training for interested students in such skills as:

Scenery design and construction
Script writing
Stage lighting
Acting
Voice training
Costuming
Staging

You might find that materials and equipment can also come from volunteer sources through contacts made by school volunteers.

MUSIC AND DANCE EXPERIENCES WITH VOLUNTEER AID

In Darien, Connecticut, volunteers conduct a successful program called *Music for Youth*. Ensemble groups and soloists are brought to the school to introduce children to the experience of hearing great music performed well. In addition to hearing the performance, the music and the instruments are often discussed and the children have an opportunity to ask questions.

Through an organizational pattern as outlined above and through appropriate fund raising, this kind of program can do much to develop a love for music that will provide students an opportunity to enjoy countless hours of pleasure and gratification throughout their lives.

A less ambitious, but equally valuable, music appreciation program can be conducted by volunteers using records and tapes. It is important that this kind of program be conducted by volunteers who are not only knowledgeable in music, but who have excellent rapport with children and are sensitive to their level of interest and interest span. Unless the proper approach is used, your efforts here can be counterproductive. This is particularly true when children become bored with, what is for them at that stage in their maturity, a tedious and uninteresting experience. Start with short, well-planned, and animated sessions. Music appreciation lessons might be correlated with work being done in other curricular areas. For instance, serious music employing melodies and themes from cowboy and folk songs might be used when studying American westward expansion. It is recommended that you encourage the volunteers who conduct music appreciation programs to be informal in their approach and to attempt to make the experience enjoyable. Assignments and tests should be discouraged.

Specialized music appreciation and performance groups or clubs can also be developed. These groups might concern themselves with such areas as jazz, classical music, rock, and soul music.

In the field of dance there are many opportunities for volunteers. Ballet and modern dance groups conducted after school hours have had great success in many schools. Square dance instruction is another extracurricular activity, as well as a regular physical education function, that can be conducted effectively by experienced practitioners who volunteer their services. A club or extracurricular activity involving social dancing can be a very helpful activity for developing self-confidence and skills in social interaction.

VOLUNTEERS AND ART EDUCATION

Most schools in the United States have come to a point where art instruction by qualified art teachers has become a reality. In many instances, instruction by professionally trained personnel takes place on a very limited basis with the regular teacher (in the case of elementary schools) sharing the instructional responsibility. Many educators consider themselves fortunate when art instruction by qualified art teachers takes place on a once-a-week basis. Whether the instruction is done by a specialist, by the classroom teacher, or under the direction of a supervisor, rarely is there sufficient time to provide programs in art appreciation and art history — again, the areas that help to provide for productive adult leisure. With the help of volunteers a very effective art appreciation program is possible. In one community where a successful volunteer art program is in existence, the following procedures are followed:

1. *Recruiting*: Parents who may or may not be actively engaged in volunteer work, but who are interested in art, are contacted. Many of them paint, sculpt, or actively engage in creative art work.

2. *Training*: The training sessions are conducted under the leadership of a volunteer leader and guided by an art educator. These sessions concern art appreciation teaching methods and the maturity and interest level of the children with whom the volunteers will work. The volunteers practice their presentations before their fellow volunteers and in the presence of the leader and professional staff members. Usually two volunteers work as a team so that one is able to conduct the lesson while the other works the slide projector or opaque projector.

3. *Equipment*: Unless each team is able to retain its own equipment, a sharing arrangement is made to prevent last-minute confusion and short supply. It is advisable to assign to the volunteers as much equipment for their exclusive use as is possible. Doing this, of course, will depend upon the amount

of equipment you have on hand and the frequency with which it will be used by the volunteers.

4. *Coordinating with the Curriculum*: Colored slide presentations augmenting the social studies curriculum are geared to intermediate and upper grade classes. For instance, a fifth grade class studying American history could see and hear presentations that depict the evolution of American art. This might start with pictures and actual examples of Indian artifacts and continue through the primitive period in American painting, the emergence of American styles, and the dominance of America in modern art.

A similar approach is taken for groups that are studying Europe, Africa, or Asia. Whatever period or part of the world being covered, there are ample opportunities to bring in appropriate art experiences. While the volunteers stress art appreciation and understanding, efforts are also made to place the art developed in the particular period and locale being studied in the context of the total social, religious, and political environment of that time. Each presentation is an interdisciplinary lesson that goes beyond a discussion of the art object and may touch upon such subjects as history, geography, religion, government, sociology, and anthropology. The student is helped to see the relevance of art to man's existence and thus acquire a better understanding of the forces that mold modern life.

5. *Acquiring Material*: Inexpensive art prints and reproductions are readily available in most communities. Prints and slides can be purchased from responsible mail order companies at a reasonable cost. Inquiries to major art museums like the National Art Museum in Washington, D.C. can result in the use of many such materials on a "permanent loan" basis with no cost to the volunteer organization.

Date _____

TO: Elementary Principals and
       Fifth and Sixth Grade Teachers
FROM: Chairman, Volunteer Art Committee

The Volunteer Art Committee is prepared to begin a series of presentations of art slide lectures in the classroom. The group is composed of members of the Public School Volunteer Program and is supervised by Miss Marjorie Shepard, Public School Coordinator of Art Education.

The program has been greeted with much enthusiasm by children and teachers of the fifth and sixth grades to whom the lectures have been given. This year, the committee will be prepared with four lectures. The committee is particularly excited about the new second semester lectures on contemporary art now in preparation. The following is the schedule of art slide presentations:

FIFTH GRADE
1. First semester (Oct. 1 — Jan. 30)   — Early American Art 17th — 19th Century
2. Second semester (Feb. 2 — May 29) — 20th Century American Art

SIXTH GRADE
1. First semester (Oct. 1 — Jan. 30)   — Renaissance Art
2. Second semester (Feb. 2 — May 29) — Contemporary Art (French Impressionism until today)

The committee has found the presentations to be most effective when teachers have remained in the classrooms during the presentations. Also, individual classes rather than large groups are preferred as student participation is always encouraged. (Programs are approximately forty minutes in length.)

Enclosed for your convenience is a very general sketch of the period covered by the first semester presentations. We hope that this will be of help to you in introducing the programs before the volunteers arrive.

If you are interested in having any of the programs in your classroom, please give a list of alternate dates and times to your principal who will in turn contact the volunteer representative in your school with this information. We will in turn confirm the date via the volunteer representative.

We are looking forward to meeting with you and your class in the near future.

SAMPLE MEMO TO PRINCIPALS AND TEACHERS
ON ART APPRECIATION PROGRAM

EARLY AMERICAN ART

Fifth Grade Slide Presentation

The group of slides used in this discussion cover two centuries of American history from 1700 to 1900. The artists represented begin with the Primitives, and include Benjamin West, John Singleton Copley, Gilbert Stuart, Winslow Homer, and conclude with Frederic Remington.

The subject matter in the picture is related to the Colonial Family, the Revolution, the Civil War, and the great Westward Movement.

We encourage the children to comment on and to participate in discussion of the slides, therefore, the showing of these slides requires the full forty minutes of class time.

The volunteer will contact the teacher to learn of the areas being covered or already covered in social studies. This information will help to make the presentations more interesting and relevant.

SAMPLE OF PROGRAM DESCRIPTION

RENAISSANCE ART

Sixth Grade Slide Presentation

The Renaissance Art Appreciation Committee introduces art from the 14th Century for the sixth grade level. During the showing of the slides, discussion and comments are encouraged — each picture is presented with a simple commentary by the volunteer. During discussions about the Renaissance or "reawakening," the following are a few of the artists shown:

> As Giotto's work introduced the Renaissance, his fresco "Christ Appears to Mary Magdalen" is the first to be discussed. At this time, the meaning of "fresco" is explained. Also during this early Italian period, Lorenzetti's picture "Saint Michael" is presented.
>
> For the 15th Century, Early Renaissance, Uccello's "The Battle of San Ramano" is well received. For exquisite colors and composition, Fra Filippo Lippi's "Adoration of the Kings" is shown. Botticelli is always exciting for the children. His "Pallas and the Centaur" creates discussion both about mythology and the beginning of perspective in artist's work.
>
> The 16th Century High Renaissance is introduced with Leonardo da Vinci's "Mona Lisa." The children's knowledge about this artist usually initiates discussion of da Vinci's contribution to science as well as to art.
>
> Presented during the Dutch period, 17th Century, are Frans Hal, Jan Vermeer, and the favorite, Rembrandt's "Aristotle Contemplating the Bust of Homer."
>
> In conclusion, a number of Michelangelo's pictures from the Sistine Chapel are shown, discussed, and most often enthusiastically received.

The volunteer will contact the teacher to learn of the areas being covered or already covered in social studies. This information will help to make the presentations more interesting and relevant.

SAMPLE OF PROGRAM DESCRIPTION

VOLUNTEERS AND LITERATURE

We have said that school volunteers who are not trained educators, but who have a keen interest and love for the fine arts, can and do make valuable contributions to the work of schools. This can also be said in the field of literature. One might feel that teachers trained in the subjects of English and literature are best equipped to teach students about their literary heritage and the literary heritage of other cultures. A strong argument can be made to support this position. When one talks to students about their studies in literature, however, one often receives negative responses. It is often an unpopular subject among intermediate, upper grade, and secondary students. One reason, perhaps, is that literature is too often a subject in which there are few opportunities for active involvement. Children rarely experience hearing stories told by gifted and skillful storytellers or hear poems and other narratives interpreted by experienced readers.

It is in the creative aspects of literature that volunteers can best serve. Writers and poets often enjoy reading and discussing their work with young people. Perhaps there are some who live in your area who would be eager to volunteer this kind of service. They don't have to be the most successful writers to be effective in discussion of literature. Professional and amateur actors can often make literature come alive for young people. A little encouragement is usually all that is needed to acquire their assistance.

Lost Art of Storytelling

People of all ages love to hear stories well told. For the young child it can be the best motivational device for acquiring reading skills. If you can find good storytellers who are willing to volunteer their services, don't let them get away! Current research has shown that children exposed to good storytelling improve their reading achievement at a faster rate than those who do not have the benefit of hearing stories.

To enhance the development of a love of good literature, you might want to schedule storytelling activities in the library or media center. It is an ideal setting. However, if this is not convenient, it can take place anywhere — the classroom, the playground, the lawn, and even in the cafeteria.

Great Books Clubs

Many schools have had great success with book discussion groups led by volunteers. This is an activity that can be done by many. The volunteer does not need experience as a writer, performer, or teacher, he only needs a love of reading.

When organizing such programs, be sure to select volunteers who have good rapport with children. Membership in book discussion groups should be voluntary; mandatory membership can create a dislike for reading great works and should be discouraged. The discussion leader should attempt to make the experience as pleasant as possible. If a participant falls behind in the reading, the volunteer should not express annoyance. Stimulating discussions will encourage him to keep up in order to gain more personal satisfaction in future sessions. The volunteer group leader must resist increasing the reading load, formal testing, or giving follow-up assignments unless they are eagerly desired by the children. Even the brightest student will resent too many infringements on his time. It must always be remembered that the main goal of a great books discussion group is to foster a love of reading.

CONCLUSION

The ways in which volunteers can make schools more productive in promoting life-long skills and interest in the creative arts are endless. We have covered only some of them. Even the most creative and hardest working educators cannot always be expert in such fields as theater production, creative writing, poetry, ballet, and modern dance. With the help of willing volunteer workers, new worlds can be opened for many. We, who work with children, must strive to expose them to those members of society who have special gifts and are willing to share them.

Developing Volunteer Community Resources / **11**

Every community, no matter what its size, has among its population people with varied skills, talents, interests, and experiences. These people have something to offer in the schools as resource persons. Lawyers, doctors, mechanics, hobbyists, machinists, collectors, nurses, and homemakers all have special skills that can be called upon to enrich the learning experiences of your students. As you seek resource people to come into the classroom, you will find that there are many sources from which to choose.

Many citizens are most willing and even eager to visit schools and share their life experiences with students. They are equipped with expertise in a variety of areas and bring with them the accumulation of many years of experience.

The task of the administrator or volunteer leader is to identify these people, compile an easy-to-use directory, and encourage teachers to invite these people into their classrooms.

In this chapter are several suggestions for accomplishing this task. Included are methods for compiling a list of resource people and sample forms to be sent to various members of the community.

RECRUITING COMMUNITY RESOURCE PEOPLE

As you prepare to compile a list of resource people from your community, you must be aware of the various organizations that may be helpful to you. These groups frequently represent a good cross section of your school district. It is a good practice to address your correspondence to the chairman or president of the organization. The letter should contain a brief explanation of the volunteer resource program and indicate the type of skills and experience that are requested. A sample letter appears in this chapter.

Some of the organizations from which you might seek assistance are:

1. Local Chamber of Commerce
2. Local Service Organizations
   a. Kiwanis Clubs
   b. Rotary Clubs
   c. Lions Clubs
   d. Exchange Clubs
3. Trade Associations
   a. Merchant's Organizations
   b. Retailer's Organizations
4. Labor Unions
5. Professional Organizations
   a. Bar Association
   b. Medical Association
   c. Dental Association
   d. Architect's Organizations
   e. Nurse's Associations
6. Local Industries
7. Hobby Groups
8. Golden Age Clubs
9. Women's Groups

Chamber of Commerce

The Chamber of Commerce could be a primary source of information since they list among their members most of the leading local business and industrial organizations. The leadership of the Chamber is usually most anxious to cooper-

Dear Mr. Chairman,

We are presently in the process of preparing a list of resource people who would be willing to come into the schools and share their talents and experiences with us. A resource person is anyone with a job skill, hobby, talent, or travel experience. He might be an electrician, artist, ham radio operator, or tourist. We have found that the students benefit greatly from the exposure to people willing to come to the classrooms to discuss their special interests.

It would be most helpful to us if you would mention this program to your membership at your next meeting. Enclosed are some questionnaires they can fill out and return to us if they are interested in taking part in the program.

Thank you for your kind attention to this request.

Sincerely,

John White
Principal

SAMPLE LETTER REQUESTING RESOURCE PEOPLE

ate and could be helpful to you as you compile your list of resource people.

Service Organizations

Service organizations, as is implicit in their name, seek to become involved in community-help projects. They take a great interest in schools and could be most helpful in preparing a list of resources. Since these groups meet on a weekly basis, an appeal to members through a club official would net quick results. Among the club membership are people with various business and professional backgrounds. Service club members may possess a variety of skills and frequently are well-traveled individuals.

Trade Associations

These groups would include wholesale and retail merchants with expertise in their field. Many of these merchants are willing to come into schools and discuss their role in the community.

You might contact association officials or work directly with the individual businessman.

Labor Unions

The labor unions represent a large cross section of skilled laborers and craftsmen. These groups have officers and you could contact them to request member participation in your resource program. If you institute a career education program as part of your curriculum, it is important that you involve members of the various unions to discuss the occupations they represent.

Professional Organizations

These organizations include doctors, lawyers, dentists, nurses, architects, and others. Members of the medical groups are often most willing to come into schools and conduct health programs and discussions relating to their professions. Many schools call upon dentists to help the youngsters learn the techniques of good dental hygiene.

Lawyers are frequently called upon to take part in drug education programs, as well as to discuss the work of the courts and legislative bodies.

Architects can contribute in many ways — as part of the art curriculum, in career education programs, in the study of community planning and development, and in the study of building design.

Local Industry

Local industry is another important resource. Local factories contain many potential volunteers with something special to bring to the classroom. The personnel director has access to information regarding employees and often is aware of their special skills or interests. Some industrial plants willingly grant employees time off to engage in public relations. School volunteer work by employees can be good public relations for local firms.

Hobby Groups

Most communities have hobby groups that meet regularly. These groups may include the following: stamp and coin collecting clubs, model builders, sewing circles, craft and needlework groups, cooking clubs, ski clubs, hot rod, skin diving, flying, and sailing clubs. These organizations usually have officers. The president or chairman is a good source to contact to request that a club member visit the school to work with youngsters in their speciality. Often these groups have presentations that include samples of their hobby skills. These visits are always popular with the youngsters and sometimes lead to a lifetime interest on the part of the students.

Golden Age Clubs

Members of Golden Age Clubs are in a unique position to be of service to the schools. Frequently, a large percentage of the membership is retired. These people often represent a wide variety of skills and experience. They also have time available to visit schools and share their knowledge with the students. Golden Age Clubs are often searching for new activities for the group and would most likely be willing to do volunteer work in the schools.

Women's Groups

Women's groups are usually service oriented and members are obligated to volunteer for a certain amount of time each year. By contacting these groups, you may find a large source of skilled and willing helpers to come into the classroom. Many of the club members will have a business or professional background and be skilled in domestic science as well.

COMPILING A LIST OF RESOURCE PEOPLE

The process of compiling a list of resource people requires some effort on your part to make the necessary contacts. You must prepare a good instrument for this purpose. A questionnaire is one technique frequently utilized in gathering information for a resource file. The questionnaire must be uncomplicated and short. The items should contain requests for name, phone number, special skills, experience or travel, length of presentation, and time and days of availability. You should also determine the amount of prior notice needed when requesting the service of the resource person. These questionnaires are sent to the key people in the organizations discussed previously. A sample questionnaire follows.

Name _____

Address _____

Phone Number _____

Special Skill _____

Presentation Format

    Lecture _____

    Demonstration _____

    Slides _____

    Display _____

    Other _____

Time of Availability _____

Amount of prior notice required _____

Do we need to supply anything for your visit?

    Projector _____

    Tape Recorder _____

    Phonograph _____

    Art Supplies_____

    Other_____

SAMPLE QUESTIONNAIRE

Another method you may employ is to send the card that you choose to use in your card file. The card has blanks for the information that you need to know. The resource person is requested to complete the card and return it to you. The card may then be dated and placed directly in the file for future use.

Date Entered — 9/25/74

Special Skill —— Artist
Name —— John Jones
Address —— 10 School Street, Monterey
Phone —— 372-1371
Time Available —— Wednesday a.m. — 9 to 12.
Material Required —— Art Supplies, Tape Recorder
Prior Notice —— one week

SAMPLE CARD FOR RESOURCE FILE

The card file is most useful if you arrange resources in categories based upon such items as: skills (glass blowing, leather work), talents (violinist, creative dance), occupations (welder, dentist), and so on, rather than by names of individuals. This enables the teacher to quickly refer to the file to find a particular type of resource person for the program of study underway.

The card file can be categorized and printed in list form. The advantage of doing this is that each teacher can be provided with a copy of the resources available.

Once you complete the file, it must be updated periodically. Additions and deletions must be dealt with and the master list revised to keep it current. As you become aware of people who are no longer available, their names should be removed. It is a good idea to update your list every year or two by sending out repeat questionnaires to your resources.

A resource list has little value if it is not used by the teachers. They should be encouraged to make the most of these community volunteers. A person whose name appears on the list but is never invited to come to the school will be less anxious to return a repeat questionnaire.

CAREER EDUCATION PROGRAMS

In recent years new emphasis has been placed on the reorganization of school curricula to accommodate more meaningful career education. It is recognized that many of our students leave school without salable job skills and with misconceptions regarding the world of work. Many school boards are revising their policies to incorporate a broader program of vocational preparation.

Volunteers, as experts in various fields of endeavor, can give the students valid insights regarding the many job opportunities awaiting them. You could invite these volunteers into the classroom to discuss their work and to answer questions for the students. By inviting several people with various occupational backgrounds, you can provide your students with an excellent overview of the world of work.

The volunteers can be called upon to conduct seminars as a part of a career education workshop. These workshops are designed to enable the students to meet with people from various occupations.

Another aspect of career education is to have students visit factories, offices, and other places of business. Your resource file would be most helpful in providing you with the names of some key people to contact and arrange for these visits. A field trip of this nature is an excellent supplement to classroom discussion.

Skilled volunteers can be invited to participate in industrial arts and business education programs. Under the direction of the teacher, volunteers could give students help as they are developing job skills in carpentry, electricity, plumbing, typing, key punch operating, and the like.

As career education assumes a more prominent role in the total scheme of school programs, it will be essential to include community resource people in the instructional process.

RESOURCE PEOPLE IN ACTIVITY GROUPS
AND HOBBY CLUBS

Activity groups meeting on a regularly scheduled basis as a part of the school program help to enliven studies for the students. In planning for these meetings, you are really only limited by the amount of time you wish to devote to them. The choice of hobbies or activities is determined by student interest and teacher skills. If their interests are such that no teacher is available with suitable skills, you can turn to your resource file to find a group leader. The group leader works cooperatively with a teacher to plan and conduct group meetings and activities.

Topics for Hobby and Activity Groups

It is highly unlikely that any two schools surveying the skills and interests of the students, teachers, and resource people would come up with the same hobby and activity groups, therefore, any discussion of specific topics is purely for purposes of demonstration. Some suggested topics for activities and suggested group goals are listed below:

1. *Photography Club* — Study of equipment, picture taking, photography contests, film making.
2. *Chess Club* — Study of the game, competitions.
3. *Sewing Club* — Study of fashions, design, tailoring, pattern alterations.
4. *Dramatics Club* — Play production, set design, study of drama.
5. *Art Club* — Mediums of artistic expression, art show.
6. *Archaeology Club* — Study of archaeology, establishment of a "dig" near the school.
7. *Gymnastics Club* — Study of gymnastics, demonstrations.

Some Suggested Hobby Groups

1. *Model Airplane Clubs* — Building and flying model airplanes, demonstrations.
2. *Coin Clubs* — Study, collect, and trade coins.
3. *Stamp Clubs* — Study, collect, and trade stamps.
4. *Craft Clubs* — Pottery, candle making, decoupage, origami.
5. *Woodworking Clubs* — Making and finishing wooden articles.

VISITING AUTHORS AND ARTISTS PROGRAM

Most towns have residing within or near their environs people who have earned recognition in writing and art. Some of these people may appear in your resource file after you have completed your survey. If they do not, you may have to recruit them by direct contact.

The concept of a visiting artist and author program is based on a series of mini-lessons conducted by practicing artists and authors. The artist visits the classroom and teaches a lesson based on his speciality, i.e., cartooning, oils, etc. This lesson may be completed in one visit or may require several visits. The same procedure is used with authors. In a series of lessons, they might cover such topics as short stories, magazine articles, or research techniques.

In this type of a program the students benefit by having direct contact with successful artists and authors. They learn from experts and are able to engage them in dialogue. This concept is also applicable to programs featuring other experts in the creative or performing arts — musicians, actors, dancers, or any other in the entertainment field.

SOME SUGGESTED RESOURCE PEOPLE

There are, in addition to those previously mentioned, other types of individuals with various interests and experiences. Each of them has the potential to help motivate students and to spark their desire for learning. Listed below are some suggested resources for you to consider:

1. Returned Peace Corps volunteers
2. Retired military men
3. Retired foreign service personnel
4. Missionaries
5. Travel agents
6. Local newspapermen
7. Local radio personalities
8. Foreign exchange students
9. Policemen
10. Firemen

The people listed in 1-5 above are usually experienced in traveling or living in foreign countries. Frequently, they have an interesting collection of pictures and artifacts gathered while visiting overseas. Students enjoy a visit from these people and benefit from listening to their experiences.

Others on the list have training that is of interest to the students. Safety programs should include a presentation by a representative of the police department. Firemen are willing to come to the schools and demonstrate some of their equipment. They also provide information on improving fire safety in the home.

Successful Use of Volunteers and Teacher Aides in Innovative School Programs / 12

One of the most common criticisms of modern schools and their curricula is that they are too frequently irrelevant in today's world. We hear much about the open classroom, the free school, differentiated staffing, and such concepts as the British Infant School. Indeed, one of the most profound innovations to receive widespread recognition is the use of volunteers and teacher aides. Using volunteers and teacher aides is also an important part of the many current innovative plans in operation.

Part of the reason for the growth of teacher-aide and volunteer programs is inspired by the need to provide inexpensive relief time for duty-free teacher lunch hours and planning periods. While this is a valid concern in light of successes experienced by teacher organizations in their negotiations with school boards, there is more important cause for the rise in the use of teacher aides and volunteers — the improvement of instruction and individualized learning. The uses for volunteers and teacher aides will expand and move in new directions. They will be an important ingredient in many innovative programs, whatever their goals. This chapter will be devoted to some of the ways in which they can be used for the successful achievement of these goals.

TEACHER AIDES AND VOLUNTEERS
IN OPEN CLASSROOMS

Much has been said and written about the "open classroom" approach to instruction. In the methodology of open classrooms, the emphasis is on better learning in concert with better instruction. Greater attempts are made to make the student more actively involved in the work in which he participates. He becomes an integral part of the planning of the activities in which he engages and does much of his work individually or in small groups.

This approach does much to make school more relevant and meaningful to the students. To run efficiently, however, open classrooms need capable teachers who can quickly adjust to changes while maintaining good organizational skills. Care must be taken to monitor the progress of each student and provide the necessary guidance and instruction to insure an appropriate level of achievement. Extra pairs of hands to aid the professional staff members in these endeavors become invaluable.

Aides assigned to open classrooms must be flexible, in addition to being skillful at helping children. You might find that, like some teachers, aides who are successful in traditional classrooms may not be suited to the open classroom methodology. It is difficult for some to work without schedules and an established routine. A multitude of activities taking place at the same time causes confusion and frustration. With patience and understanding some will adjust to new methods and procedures — others may not. You need to select aides carefully for assignments to open classrooms and provide them with as much pretraining and orientation as time permits to insure success.

AIDES IN TEAM TEACHING

Various forms of team teaching have been in practice for a number of years. A variation of team teaching identified as differentiated staffing is presently receiving much attention.

Team-teaching programs take into consideration the varying ability, strengths, and weaknesses of individual teachers. Some teachers are better at language arts instruction than math instruction. Some have highly refined skills in organization and planning; others are creative and able to motivate their students to do exceptional work. A team-teaching organizational approach permits teachers to better capitalize on their special talents. Through careful planning and scheduling, individual teachers concentrate on specific units of study. Children are often grouped and regrouped to receive instruction from two or more teachers or aides according to the needs and interests of the students.

The Role of Teacher Aides and Volunteers in Differentiated Staffing

In a differentiated staffing plan, the team operates in much the same manner as outlined above. However, a member of the team is selected to serve as a team leader or master teacher. Other gradations of staff may also exist. Much of the leadership in planning and scheduling comes from the team leader who may often be a quasi-supervisor as well as a teacher in the team.

In many team-teaching organizational plans, particularly differentiated staffing, aides are a definite part of the organization and play an important role. They, too, are called upon to exercise their talents to the fullest. Under the guidance of the professional staff, they assist and monitor progress in individual and small group projects. They tutor individuals in skill development, as well as many other activities, to help the teachers and the students.

An important consideration in team teaching is good communication between the staff members involved. Often daily meetings of one sort or another are needed in order to have a smooth and efficient operation. The aide is a valuable resource here. She can relieve teachers for brief times during the day to facilitate this much needed communication.

Whenever possible, teacher aides should be included

in team planning sessions. Their advice based on their experience with individual children can be valuable. The more aides become a vital part of the team, the better will be your chances for a successful program.

In many team-teaching plans employing teacher aides, it becomes difficult for visitors to differentiate the aides from the professional staff members. When this occurs, it is often an indication that the program is achieving success. With thoughtful selection and good training, aides become very valuable members of the team. This is not an outcome that should cause excessive concern or skepticism to professionals. It must be remembered that it is through creative and effective guidance and supervision on the part of the professional that this kind of success on the part of aides can be achieved.

Because the team members will eventually work closely with the aides, it is wise to have the members of a team play a major role in interviewing and selecting candidates for team teacher-aide positions.

AIDES AND VOLUNTEERS IN BRITISH
INFANT SCHOOL PLANS

British Infant School programs, modeled after some of the more progressive schools in Great Britain, are gaining in interest in the United States. Many of the principles in this plan have been discussed in the previous chapters that dealt with modern approaches in preschool and primary grades and individualized instruction. In short, the British Infant School attempts to make the best use of the young child's natural inquisitive and self-motivating nature. Each child is encouraged to pursue his interest and to learn through natural discovery. Attempts are made to facilitate programs for individual children as much as possible instead of for whole classes or groups.

An important feature of British Infant School classrooms is the physical appearance and arrangement. Obviously, a program geared to meet individual needs of twenty-five or more children requires the introduction and use of many materials. Most of these materials are prepared by the children and staff. The materials are organized at various places in the classroom. When children are finished with a task, they are permitted to go to another interest center to engage in another activity.

The philosophy behind the practice in schools of this type is not new. Claims of success where similar attempts in the past have failed are said to result where close monitoring of the children's progress takes place. While it appears that children have greater opportunity to do as they wish, they are given as much guidance and instruction as needed to insure the proper skill development. They are encouraged to stay with their projects until they are satisfactorily completed and discouraged from using valuable time on less productive or less meaningful activities.

Teacher aides and volunteers can be of immeasurable assistance in programs such as British Infant School plans. Keeping the interest centers in good order is a task that requires an extra pair of hands. Monitoring the progress of young children also necessitates constant attention. Aides and volunteers can do this valuable service without requiring a great amount of the professional's time or supervision. The task of helping children to prepare their own materials can also be assigned to them.

When using volunteers and aides to help children prepare materials, it is advisable to encourage maximum participation by the children. The children will profit most from meaningful discovery when they have had a maximum of involvement.

The value of volunteers should not be underestimated in such programs that attempt to focus keenly on individualization. Because the interests of each child are carefully considered to provide a high level of stimulation and motivation, the special talents of members of your volunteer group can be of immense service. The young child who has a special interest in such things as doll costumes, coins, or Indians might be paired with a volunteer with similar interests. With direction from the teacher, such a volunteer could do much to further the child's interest and develop academic skills as a natural outgrowth of pursuing such interests.

OPEN SPACE SCHOOLS

An increasing number of new school buildings on both the elementary and secondary levels are being constructed without interior walls. Areas with enough floor space to house as many as two hundred or more students are being used as a single unit with some movable partitions that can be used for chalkboards, storage, and display.

The physical features of these schools tend to make them more conducive to a variety of innovative school approaches. In them you may find programs that highlight specific innovations or, more likely, a combination of several innovations. They include such concepts as individualized learning and instruction, team teaching, differentiated staffing, multiage grouping, independent study, nongradedness, and open classrooms.

In these schools, teacher aides and volunteers are almost always included in its staffing pattern. One such school, the Stadley Rough Elementary School in Danbury, Connecticut, successfully employed nine teacher aides and used more than eighty volunteers to serve a student enrollment of 500 during its first year in operation. If "schools without walls" become commonplace, it would be hard to imagine schools and school districts without teacher aides and volunteers.

The ways in which aides and volunteers are used in open space schools have been discussed in those pages devoted to the various concepts employed in these schools. A major factor, however, seems to be evident at this time — aides and volunteers tend to fit naturally into the staffing arrangement and procedures for operating in open space schools. If your community moves in the direction of open space schools, be sure to devote as much time and effort as possible to preservice and in-service training for aides and volunteers. Whenever possible, involve the teaching staff in the selection, as well as the training process.

VOLUNTEERS AND TEACHER AIDES
IN ENVIRONMENTAL EDUCATION PROGRAMS

Ecologists and other scientists have been alerting us to the dangers of pollution and excessive use of our natural resources. Although the warnings have been expressed for many years, it is only within recent years that large segments of society and governmental leaders have given serious consideration to the environmental crisis that confronts the whole world. When issues of such magnitude capture the imagination and concern of millions, a discussion of the role of the school becomes inevitable.

In the cause of environmental protection most agree that the youth of the nation will play a major role in determining the course of the future. It is the present generation of youth who will be the future producers and consumers in a world inhabited by more people than ever have existed at a single time throughout the ages. If the crisis is to subside, new modes of consumption and means of conserving goods and resources will need to be devised. Men will have to discover forms of energy that pollute the environment less than the present forms and learn ways to reuse materials efficiently.

To effectively institute programs in environmental education, schools will need the help of many in the communities. Volunteers who are knowledgeable in ecology and conservation can be used to show the effects of improper land, water, and forest use. Other volunteers can assist in making the necessary transportation and other physical arrangements needed to conduct a comprehensive environmental program.

Local groups like garden clubs, museum staffs, nature centers, physicians, conservation commissions, and many other business and professional groups are excellent sources of expertise and, in some instances, funds to conduct meaningful programs. Some garden clubs have done such things as provide scholarships for teachers to pursue courses in nature study, conservation, and ecology. Some have helped schools to develop nature centers for school use and have assisted teachers and students in planting trees and shrubs on school grounds. Volunteer groups and individuals have developed excellent audio-visual presentations and demonstrations for classrooms and school-wide programs.

Many schools are finding the help of volunteers of great value in efforts on behalf of such conservation measures as recycling drives. Involving young people in work activities on these projects by collecting and preparing used paper, cans, and bottles for recycling is a valuable community service, and a valid educational experience in preserving our natural resources. Attention is also brought to many families and the community at large regarding the importance of immediate action to avert a widening environmental crisis.

VOLUNTEERS AID DRUG EDUCATION

Formal drug education programs are springing up all over the country to help combat the growing problem of drug abuse and addiction. Efforts are being made to avert such abuse by demonstrating the harmful effects of unwarranted drug use in ways that are relevant and truly meaningful. Because educators rarely have firsthand experience with drug abuse, they often suffer a lack of credibility with students. Appropriate volunteers often do not have such problems and can be of valuable help. Using volunteers who were formerly drug dependent, doctors who treat drug patients, or law-enforcement personnel who deal with crime associated with drug use can be most beneficial to your drug education program.

A community that successfully conducts volunteer programs in the schools will have an easier job of launching a meaningful drug program. Volunteers who engage in other activities may be an excellent source for recruiting those who can be helpful in classroom work in drug education. They can also help to develop in-service programs for teachers on this vital subject. We have talked about various in-service training plans for aides and volunteers to help teachers. In this area, appropriate members of the community can help to train teachers to be knowledgeable of the forces that lead individuals to drug abuse, to learn about the effects of drugs on health, and to discover the complex antisocial results of drug abuse. Teachers, like others in the community, may be victims of misunderstandings and misinformation concerning drugs, since drug abuse has only recently become recognized as a social problem that has directly or indirectly affected millions of people throughout the world. There is much to learn about this problem. We in education cannot begin to solve this problem without the voluntary help of many from all walks of life.

FAMILY LIFE EDUCATION

In spite of the many objections to the sexual aspects of family life programs, there continues to be interest in this vital subject. Consider a role for volunteers when you discuss ways to institute or improve such programs.

Not only will such volunteers from the medical and religious fields provide special expertise, they will provide valuable assistance to you when there is a need for convincing the community that your program has been carefully planned and intelligently executed.

CONCLUSION

The possibilities for teacher aides and volunteers in programs that may be new or innovative for your community are many. In some programs they play an integral and vital role. In many communities volunteers and aides have been so effective in making new programs succeed that funds that were formerly unavailable were provided to continue and broaden the innovative offerings of schools. There is a wealth of free and inexpensive assistance available to those who desire to improve their efforts on behalf of children. Seek and you shall find!

Recognizing and Evaluating Volunteer and Teacher-Aide Programs / **13**

It is important that you recognize the contribution volunteers have made to the school program. It is also very important for the volunteers to know you are appreciative of their efforts on behalf of the students. In view of this, you may wish to plan a social function for the purpose of thanking the volunteers.

You may choose a variety of methods to honor the volunteers. Foremost among these is the word of thanks or "pat on the back" that you give to the volunteers on a day-to-day basis. They should not have to wait until the annual awards function before receiving recognition.

A tea held after school is another way in which the teachers can show their appreciation for the volunteer help. Another popular affair is to honor the volunteers at a P.T.A. meeting. You might also consider a brief news article in the local paper praising the volunteers for their service.

Other means of expressing appreciation are:

1. Personal thank you letters.
2. Invitations to return for further service.
3. Seeking suggestions for improving service from the volunteer.
4. A story in the school newsletter.
5. A special award ceremony.

A sample letter that includes a thank you as well as an invitation to a tea follows.

[NAME OF SCHOOL]
[City and State]

Date

Dear Parent Volunteer:

On behalf of the students and faculty of King Street School, I would like to invite you to a tea on Tuesday, June 6, 1973, at 3:15 p.m. in the cafeteria.

The purpose of this occasion is to enable us to extend to you our gratitude for the help you have provided us this year. The many hours you have devoted to assisting students and teachers in the learning process have enriched our school program.

I certainly hope you will be able to attend. We are looking forward to meeting with you.

To help us with our planning, please complete the attached form and return it to the school office. Thank you.

Sincerely,

_____
Principal

I will _____ will not _____ be able to attend.

_____
Parent Volunteer

SAMPLE LETTER

SPECIAL AWARD CEREMONY

The special award ceremony may be planned as part of the tea or P.T.A. meeting. The ceremony should include remarks by a school official, teacher representative, and chairman of parent volunteers. Emphasis should be placed on the volunteers' dedication to the service of youngsters, dependability, sense of responsibility, and for their patience and understanding.

A certificate of appreciation given to each volunteer is a popular technique for honoring these dedicated people. This certificate need not be elaborate and can be made in the school of readily available materials. (A sample certificate follows.)

PARENT VOLUNTEER CERTIFICATE OF OUTSTANDING DEDICATION

𝒯he students and staff of King Street School extend their appreciation to _____ for many hours of service provided throughout the year. Please accept our sincere thanks.

KING STREET SCHOOL
DANBURY, CONN.
19 __

SAMPLE CERTIFICATE

EVALUATING YOUR VOLUNTEER PROGRAM

You must continually evaluate your program in order to determine if it is accomplishing its basic purpose. The process of evaluation should be ongoing so that modifications can be made as they are needed, rather than at the end of the school year.

The teacher will have the primary responsibility for evaluating volunteer performance since he works most directly with this person. He should confer with the volunteer and offer praise as well as suggestions for improvement. If a volunteer does not work out in a particular classroom, the volunteer leader or principal should be contacted to make a change of assignment.

You should request information from the teachers regarding the volunteer program. Some questions that you may ask them are:

1. Are the volunteers providing you with the kind of service you anticipated when you requested them?
2. Have the volunteers been cooperative in working with you?
3. Do you feel you would like further workshops on the use of volunteers?
4. Would you like the volunteer program continued during the next school year?

TEACHER EVALUATIONS

Do the Volunteers Provide Service?

It is important that the teachers who work with volunteers are satisfied with the services the volunteers provide. They must be confident that the volunteers or aides are capable of performing the tasks to which they are assigned. Volunteers who do not like the type of work they are doing in one classroom should be reassigned to another. Every effort should be made to provide the teacher with a volunteer or aide who meets the needs of the class.

Do the Volunteers Cooperate?

If the team of professionals and nonprofessionals is to achieve success, there must be good communication as well as cooperation. The paraprofessional must look to the teacher to provide the necessary educational leadership. The teacher must treat the volunteer or aide with dignity and respect. The tasks asked of the volunteer must be reasonable and within their capabilities. They, in turn, must be willing to accept the assignment given to them.

Do Teachers Need Workshops?

A workshop for the teachers designed to help them use volunteers more effectively will improve the program. The teachers should be the primary determinants of the content of the workshops. These sessions should be based on skills that will result in effective and efficient use of the nonprofessionals who work with them in the classroom.

Do Teachers Want to Continue the Volunteer Program?

This is the most significant question in the evaluation process. The best indication of the success of the program is when the professional staff expresses enthusiasm for the program. This enthusiasm and a desire to see the program expand will inevitably occur when good planning and training take place.

CHAIRMAN EVALUATION

The chairman of volunteers should be asked to evaluate the program as the administrative leader of the nonprofessionals. Some criteria he must keep in mind are:

1. The dependability and punctuality of individual volunteers.
2. The strengths and weaknesses of the recruiting technique used in obtaining volunteers.
3. The quality of the communication among the staff, the volunteer, and the administrators.
4. The effectiveness of the volunteer training program in preparing the volunteers for their work in the classroom.

Dependability and Punctuality of Volunteers

The chairman of volunteers must be cognizant of the performance of each of the volunteers. A good volunteer must be dependable and regular in attendance. Tardiness on the part of the volunteer is also undesirable because of the disruptive nature of late entry into the classroom. The chairman of volunteers should discuss the performance of each volunteer with the teacher and, when necessary, encourage errant people to improve.

The Recruiting Program

A major function of the chairman is to recruit volunteers to work in the schools. These recruiting techniques should be constantly revised and modified. Those methods that prove to be successful can be continued, while those that are not effective should be eliminated. Consulting with volunteers on the techniques that attracted them can be very helpful.

Quality of Communication

It is most important to maintain good open channels of communication between the principals involved. Any problems that arise should be discussed by those who are in a position to help solve them. The chairman can often act as an intermediary in handling problems that may occur between a volunteer and a teacher.

Effectiveness of Training Program

An ongoing appraisal of the effectiveness of the training program is essential. Teachers and the volunteers are in the best position to provide the chairman with feedback on the strengths and weaknesses of their preparation. The success of the volunteer program is dependent to a large extend upon the quality of training. If you can find ways to improve and upgrade the training of volunteers, it will be reflected in the performance in the classroom.

VOLUNTEER EVALUATION

The volunteer, as one of the principals in the program, should be asked to evaluate his own performance as well as to give his views on the overall program. It is important to do this for two reasons: (1) It indicates that you have respect for his judgment and are interested in any suggestions he might have; (2) Self-evaluation requires reflection on the

part of the individual and helps him toward self-improvement.
Some questions that may be asked of the volunteer are:

1. Do you feel that you have achieved your goals as a
   volunteer?
2. What are your greatest strengths as a volunteer?
3. In what areas do you feel you need to improve?
4. In your opinion, in what ways can the school volunteer program be improved?

Achievement of Goals

During the training program the volunteers were encouraged to establish goals for themselves. It is a good practice to ask the volunteer to reflect upon these goals as they
work in the classroom. The goals will provide the volunteer
with guidance and a measure upon which they can evaluate
their own performance. The volunteer should determine
whether or not he has accomplished what he intended during
his involvement in the school program.

The volunteer should try to determine his strengths in
his role as a volunteer. With this insight, the volunteer can
capitalize on his skills and work more effectively in the
classroom. Self-assessment is an important aspect of any
evaluative process. Those who can do this realistically will
be better able to apply themselves to their role as a volunteer.

Areas in Need of Personal Improvement

The volunteer should be aware of areas that need to
be improved. This is of particular significance where they
are working directly with students. Self-evaluation is an important aspect of the improvement of performance. An
accurate understanding of individual strengths and weaknesses precedes the actual process of sharpening one's skills.

Improvement of the School Volunteer Program

How the program might be improved is a question that
might be asked of all participants in the volunteer program.
It is very helpful to solicit opinions from the volunteers

since they are involved at the grass roots level. The volunteers should be encouraged to offer constructive criticism and their suggestions should be put into practice whenever possible.

ADMINISTRATOR EVALUATION

The school administrator must also assess the volunteer program and use this assessment as a basis for change when change is called for. The administrator must keep in mind the needs of the students as the overriding criterion upon which to base his decision. He must be cognizant of the relationship between the teachers and volunteers. Most of all, the administrator must determine whether the program is making a positive contribution to the improvement of instruction; then he should seek ways of expanding and improving it.

The school administrator should answer the following questions:

1. Do you feel that the recruiting procedures are satisfactory?
2. Does the training program provide effective volunteers?
3. Is the volunteer program meeting the needs of the teachers and their students?
4. Is the volunteer program providing good public relations for the school?
5. Is the program one that should be continued in the school?

Assessing Recruiting Procedures

A complete assessment of the recruiting techniques would help to determine the most effective methods. The administrator is in the best position to observe the results of the recruiting program. He must confer with the chairman of volunteers in attempting to create new and effective procedures for bringing volunteers into the school program.

Training Program Effectiveness

The performance of the volunteers is the best indication of the effectiveness of the training they received. If the administrator determines that the volunteers need help in certain areas, this knowledge should be reflected in modification of the training program. Once again, the administrator should seek the cooperation of the chairman of volunteers and the volunteers themselves to evaluate the effect of the training program.

Meeting the Needs of Students and Volunteers

Do the volunteers have a significant role in helping the teachers to achieve their educational objectives? Is there evidence that individual students are benefiting from the help these nonprofessionals provide them? Have the volunteers been able to provide the specific help that the teachers initially requested? If the answers to these questions are largely affirmative, you can be assured that the program is a worthwhile activity.

Public Relations

Good public relations can be a major fringe benefit of a volunteer program. If the volunteers are enjoying their work in the school, they will be purveyors of good tidings to the community. You should encourage occasional newspaper stories on the activities of volunteers. It is also a good practice to include an article or two about the volunteers in the school in home newsletters. If good public relations do not accrue as a result of using volunteers, efforts should be made to determine the reason for this.

Continuance of the Program

Whether or not the program should be continued can be decided after you have evaluated the total program and determined its contribution to effective instruction in your school. If you take reasonable care when embarking on volunteer or teacher-aide programs, the answer most assuredly will be a resounding yes!

APPENDIX I

SAMPLE BY-LAWS FOR A SCHOOL VOLUNTEER PROGRAM

BY-LAWS

PUBLIC SCHOOL VOLUNTEER PROGRAM INC.

ARTICLE I

Section 1. ANNUAL MEETING
The annual meeting of the Members of the Corporation shall be held at such time and place each year in the month of May as the Board of Directors shall determine. The Secretary shall give at least ten days' notice in writing to all Members of the Corporation.

Section 2. SPECIAL MEETING
Special meetings of Members may be called at any time by a majority of the Directors, or by a petition signed by 15 Members. The Secretary shall give notice of the Special Meeting as above.

Section 3. QUORUM
The presence of 15% of the Members shall constitute a quorum.

ARTICLE II — DIRECTORS

Section 1. BOARD OF DIRECTORS
The Board of Directors shall be composed of no more than 20 nor less than 5 persons who are Members of the Corporation.

Section 2. ELECTION
The Board of Directors shall be elected by the Members present at the annual meeting.

Section 3. TERM OF OFFICE
The term of office of each director shall be for one year.

Section 4. DUTIES
The Board of Directors shall have the control and general management of the affairs and business of the Corporation.

Section 5. MEETINGS
The Board of Directors shall meet regularly directly following the annual meeting of the Members and at such time and place as they determine or at the call of the President or three (3) Directors on 5 days' written notice.

Section 6. VACANCIES
Vacancies in the Board occurring between annual meetings shall be filled for the unexpired term by a majority of the remaining Directors.

Section 7. QUORUM
The presence of a majority of the members shall constitute a quorum.

ARTICLE III — OFFICERS

Section 1. OFFICERS
The officers of this Corporation shall be President, Executive Vice-President, 1st Vice-President, Secretary and Treasurer.

Section 2. ELECTION
All the aforementioned officers shall be elected by the Board of Directors at its annual meeting held immediately after the meeting of Members, except for the Executive Vice-President who shall be appointed by the Superintendent of Schools. The Executive Vice-President will represent and be a member of the school administration staff.

Section 3. DUTIES

President:
The President shall preside at all meetings of the Board of Directors and Members, issue the call of the annual meeting, and special meetings, and Board meetings; appoint all committees necessary to the proper conduct of the affairs of the Corporation. Said appointments shall be

ratified by the Board of Directors at the earliest possible opportunity. The President shall be ex-officio a Member of all committees.

Executive Vice-President:
The Executive Vice-President shall be the representative of the Public School System. He shall appoint all professional co-chairman of committees.

1st Vice-President:
1st Vice-President shall assume the duties of the President in his absence, and such other duties as may be assigned by the Board.

Secretary:
The Secretary shall keep minutes of all meetings of the Members and the Board of Directors, and shall give notice of all meetings called by the Chairman.

Treasurer:
The Treasurer shall be responsible for the maintenance of records of all receipts and expenditures of the Corportion and deposit such funds in the name of the Corporation in such bank as the Board of Directors may designate. He shall be responsible for the payment of all bills presented to the Corporation. He shall submit reports on expenditures to the Board at times to be recommended by the Board.

Section 4. VACANCIES
All vacancies in any office shall be filled by the Board of Directors.

Section 5. COMPENSATION
The officers shall receive no salary or compensation.

ARTICLE IV — AUTHORITY

All activities and policies of the Corporation shall be subject to and under the jurisdiction of the Board of Education of the (City and State). In the event of any disagreement of activities or policy, the opinion of the Board of Education as set forth by the Executive Vice-President shall prevail.

ARTICLE V — SERVICE COMMITTEES

All Service Committees shall have co-chairmen, one volunteer and one professional. The volunteer shall be appointed by the President as stated in ARTICLE III, Section 3. The professional shall be appointed by the Executive Vice-President as stated in Article III, Section 3.

ARTICLE VI — AMENDMENTS

These By-Laws may be amended by the vote of the Board of Directors or by a vote of the Members at any Annual or Special Meeting. Any amendment must be approved by the Superintendent of Schools before it can become effective.

APPENDIX II

Name of School
City and State

Date_____

TO: Volunteer Storytellers
FROM: Reading Consultant
SUBJECT: Responsibilities and Procedures

1. Report to the Principal's Office before going to the library. The secretary will give you the names and room numbers of the children with whom you will be working.
2. Check the library or media center to be sure that chairs are arranged and materials ready for use.
3. Pick up children at their room. Wait for the teacher to introduce you if it is your first visit.
4. Take no disciplinary action. If a child continues to misbehave after you have requested his cooperation, return him to his teacher. She will take care of the matter.
5. After story time the children must be returned to their teacher.
6. Report to the Principal's secretary when you are ready to leave the building.
7. If for any reason you are unable to keep your appointment, call the school in the morning.

STORIES ANYONE CAN TELL*

PICTURE BOOKS
In the Forest, by Marie Hall Ets.

---

*Permission granted by Mrs. Augusta Baker, Coordinator of the Office of Children's Services, The New York Public Library.

Millions of Cats, by Wanda Gag.
The Golden Goose Book, by L. Leslie Brooke.
The Three Billy Goats Gruff, by P.C. Asbjorsen, illustrated by
    Marcia Brown.
Tikki-Tikki-Tembo, by Arlene Mosel, illustrated by Blair Lent.
Andy and the Lion, by James Daugherty.
Whistle for Willie, by Ezra Jack Keats.
Make Way for Ducklings, by Robert McCloskey.

FOLK TALES

"Molly Whuppie," "Henny Penny," "Tom Tit Tot," "Teeny-Tiny." In:
    English Folk and Fairy Tales, by Joseph Jacobs.
"The Cat on the Dovrefell," "The Giant Who Had No Heart in His
    Body." In: *East of the Sun and West of the Moon*, by P.C.
    Asbjorsen and J.E. Moe.
"The Fisherman and His Wife," "Cat and Mouse Keep House," "The
    Frog Prince." In: *Tales from Grimm*, by Wanda Gag.
"The Shepherd's Nosegay," "Mighty Mikko." In: *The Shepherd's
    Nosegay*, by Parker Fillmore; edited by Katherine Love.
"Mr. Samson Cat," "The Bun," "Snowflake." In: *The Buried Treasure*,
    selected by Eulalie Steinmetz Ross.
"The Golden Lynx," "The Princess with the Twelve Pair of Golden
    Shoes." In: *The Golden Lynx and Other Tales*, selected by
    Augusta Baker.
"Baba Yaga," "Prince Ivan, The Witch Baby, and the Little Sister of
    the Sun." In: *Old Peter's Russian Tales*, by Arthur Ransome.
"The Tiger and the Rabbit," "The Bed." In: *The Tiger and the Rabbit*,
    by Pura Belpre.
"Clever Grethel," "The Three Sillies." In: *Tales Told Again*, by Walter
    de la Mare.
"The Tinker and the Ghost," "Black Magic." In: *Three Golden Oranges*,
    by Ralph Steele Boggs and Mary Gould Davis.
"Old Fire Dragaman," "Jack and the Bean Tree." In: *The Jack Tales*,
    by Richard Chase.
"The Woodcutter of Gura," "Goat Well." In: *The Fire on the Moun-
    tain*, by Harold Courlander.

BOOKS TO READ ALOUD

It's Perfectly True and Other Stories, by Hans Christian Andersen;
    translated by Paul Leyssac.
Just So Stories, by Rudyard Kipling.

Rootabaga Stories, by Carl Sandburg.
Come Hither: A Collection of Rhymes and Poems for the Young of All Ages, compiled by Walter de la Mare.
Humorous Poetry for Children, edited by William Cole.

BOOKS ABOUT STORYTELLING
The Art of the Storyteller, by Marie L. Shedlock.
The Way of the Storyteller, by Ruth Sawyer.

Index